Corn Born

&

Corn Bread

A Collection of Southern Essays

Neal Wooten

ISBN 978-1-61225-438-8

Published by Mirror Publishing
Fort Payne, AL 35967
www.pagesofwonder.com

Printed in the USA

Table of Contents

"You can take the boy from the mountain, but not the mountain from the boy."

-Neal Wooten

Speak Southern

After living up north for the last ten years, I can tell you first hand that good old Southern words and phrases, which make perfect sense to us, confuse the heck out of Yankees. So for anyone who isn't fluent in Southernese, I reckon I'm fixin' to teach you a few things. Don't worry; learning Southernisms is as easy as falling off a log.

If it seems hard at first, hold your horses. Don't have a conniption or pitch a hissy fit. Don't fly off the handle or get your feathers all ruffled or you might feel like you got the short end of the stick and holler like a stuck pig. It doesn't take a coon's age to learn as long as you don't sit there like a bump on a log. Just stay as busy as a one-legged man in a butt-kicking contest.

But it takes longer than two shakes of a cow's tail. You can't count your chickens before they hatch or put the cart before the horse. Don't bite off more than you can chew or go off half-cocked or people will think you're too big for your britches. Remember, every dog has a few fleas but even a blind squirrel finds an acorn now and then.

So go hog wild and whole hog too. If you pay attention to my words, you'll soon be chugged full of useful expressions. But don't get cocky and let the tail wag the dog. Remember, wisdom is as scarce as hen's teeth. Don't let your mouth overload your butt or you'll be barking up the wrong tree.

Don't carry on or be a worry wart and don't act biggity. Even if you don't have a pot to pee in, just have fun with it and all your Southern friends will think you were raised in high cotton. You can catch them with their pants down and y'all will be like two peas in a pod. Your fences will be mended and you'll have no axe to grind.

Keep practicing if you've a mind to and aim to be a sweet talking thang charming the Southern Belles to accompany you to a shindig. Well I'll be; directly you'll know pert near more Southern words than old Do-Hickey who lives over yonder. You will take the cake and your friends will just stare at you and say things like "I do declare" and "Well shut my mouth."

When you get to where you can understand this entire article, you've passed. You're not a mess anymore. You can now run with the big dogs. The South is now your stomping grounds. Bless your heart. Give me some sugar and if I ain't too tore up, I'll take you muddin'.

Caterwauling

I come from a family of singers. My dad had an awesome voice. I loved to hear him sing old songs like "In Them Old Cotton Fields Back Home" or "Green Green Grass of Home" or any of Johnny Horton's classic songs like "North to Alaska" and "Six Feet Below."

My Uncle Jerry, Dad's youngest brother, was very talented. He taught himself the guitar and could play by ear, and his voice was as smooth and mellow as any famous singer. He could nail any Elvis Presley song, but my favorites to hear him sing were "Thunder Road" and "Sixteen Tons."

There are still lots of great singers in the Wooten family today and of course our cousins, the Owens, is a family rich with singers on the mountain. Some became professional singers even, especially in the gospel genre.

You may be wondering if this is just an opportunity for me to brag about my own vocal skills. Nope! I'm perhaps the only Wooten that this particular gene went way around. As they say on the mountain: "I can't carry a tune in a bucket."

Of course that didn't stop me from singing. Well, "singing" might not be the right word. "Caterwauling" I think is more accurate, which the dictionary describes as "to screech like a cat in heat."

I began singing in church when I was five. My song of choice: "One, Two, Three, The Devil's After Me." By the time I was 12, "No Tears in Heaven" and "Were You There" were the staples of my performances.

Finally, when I was about 15, I heard myself singing on a tape recorder and it scared me. How could the sound in my head be so wrong? I began to realize just how incredibly polite the members of my church had been. Just the suffering they endured hearing me sing should grant them eternal life.

I always thought God was pretty generous with me on most things except height. I think I'm a little better than average when it comes to math, art, writing, sense of humor, and maybe even in strength. But oh no, my vocal chords were not part of His grand scheme for me I guess.

I love to sing while I drive to pass time. But now I rarely go anywhere without my wife. When I start singing with her in the car, she automatically turns on the radio without even realizing she's doing it.

And when I used to have any of my nephews in the car, back when they were teenagers, I would ask them if they wanted me to sing them a song. To which they would reply, "That's all right, Uncle Neal, you can just tell us a joke."

Slow Southern Drawl

Admittedly, when I was a kid I had a very pronounced Southern dialect. And not just Southern, but Sand Mountain Southern, which means it wasn't just the accent, but it was filled with those colorful country words and phrases.

It was so bad, in fact, that when I first began college at Auburn University, people couldn't understand me. Heck, they even got my name wrong. Instead of hearing "Neal Wooten," they heard "Leo Whitten."

My dialogue was probably as rich in hillbilly verbiage as any good old boy or girl who rolled off that mountain. But there was one difference – I did not speak slowly. Not even close. From first grade through 12th, teachers often called on me to read aloud in class, and as soon as I began, my classmates started yelling. "Slow down!" I didn't even know I was going fast.

When I had been performing standup comedy for only a few months, I met one of the biggest comics on the circuit. His name was Ollie Joe Prater and he was also literally the biggest, weighing more than 400 pounds. He looked like Charlie Daniels with his hat and beard, only much larger.

Knowing I was new to comedy, Ollie Joe offered to watch my show and provide feedback. He was the first comedian, and really the only one, to offer help to a struggling newbie. After my set, he called me back to his table, peered out from under his cowboy hat, and yelled, "Slow down!" Gee, where have I heard that before?

After I had been working the comedy scene for six months, it was time to make my first demo tape. Mr. Niblett, my old science teacher, was kind enough to do the filming. When I finally watched myself on tape, all I could think was one thing -- Slow Down! I finally heard what everyone else was hearing.

So I began concentrating on speaking slower, and I actually still do that to this day. Saturday morning I gave a presentation to the Etowah County Genealogy Society and made sure to speak as slow as I could. It probably still came out faster than normal people, but folks were able to understand me.

And it's not just when I give speeches; it's in everyday conversations. Whether I'm greeting visitors at the Depot Museum, or speaking with authors on the telephone, I still have to focus on slowing down.

So if you see me out and about in town or on the mountain and we talk for a spell, and you leave thinking I was talking a mile-a-minute, know that I was still talking much slower than what comes natural to me.

I'm No City Slicker

Being a country boy from the rural South usually makes me stick out like a sore thumb in Milwaukee. Just my accent alone makes people pause as they smile and try to guess where I'm from. Most get close by guessing Georgia, Mississippi, Tennessee, or occasionally someone who clearly has no concept of the South at all will guess Texas.

And of course it's not just the accent but the words and phrases I use that raise a brow. "Ma'am" and "sir" always confuse folks, as does "please" and "thank you" most times. And other than my wife, I've yet to teach anyone what "fixin' to" means.

I know I've upset many men and women up here by not having an answer to the following questions:

"How are the Packers gonna do this year?"

"Did you watch the Packers last night?"

"Are the Packers going all the way?"

I kid you not; it's an obsession equal only to Tiger and Tide fans. There are so many green-and-yellow jackets and winter coats up here that I almost think I'm back in Sylvania. When I explain that I'm from Alabama and I only watch college football, they look like someone kicked them in the gut.

I have puzzled many a waiter and waitress by inquiring

about grits. I now know the few restaurants that carry grits, and some of them, like Denny's, serve grits but don't have them on their menus. How weird is that?

I try to represent Alabama well, but that's not always the case. Sometimes people just don't get my jokes and it leaves them with a bewildered view of my home state. Case and point was my visit last week to have my teeth cleaned.

The hygienist knew I was from Alabama and was intrigued by that. After an hour and a half of pure agony as she scraped off tartar and plaque from underneath my gums, which had been there since the Cretaceous period, she offered me a gift, since, in her own words, I had been such a good boy.

She actually said that. I guess because I didn't cry too much. She held out four brand new Oral-B toothbrushes, in four different colors, and told me to pick one. "Thanks," I said and looked them over. Then I added, "What are those?"

You should have seen the look on her face. It reminds me of a joke. "How do we know that the toothbrush was invented in Alabama?"

Answer: "Because if it had been invented anywhere else, it would be called a teethbrush."

The Way I Was Raised

This past Saturday I spoke to the DeKalb County Genealogy Society at the public library in Fort Payne, a great bunch of folks. Knowing how they loved history, I used my time to talk about the research I did for the Granny Dollar novel, and things I learned from it.

One thing that stood out to me was that Nancy (Granny Dollar) had been raised in a predominantly Cherokee environment with Native American culture. After the forced relocation, however, when Nancy was about 15, the landscape changed to a majority of white settlers, as did the culture. But Nancy never let go of her Indian way of life. Even living to the ripe old age of 106, she was still a Cherokee through-and-through.

It dawned on me that she and I have that in common. After living in the Montgomery area for 20 years and Milwaukee, Wisconsin for ten more, I'm still Sand Mountain to the bone. My accent might have faded, but I still act the same as I was taught as a kid.

One day in Milwaukee as I was driving Maggie home from work, we passed a minivan on the side of the road with a flat tire and they seemed to be having trouble changing it. Without thinking, I turned around and went back. There were several kids in the van, and the dad was trying to get the lug bolts off using that tiny wrench that comes with the vehicle.

I took out my huge four-way lug wrench that I always kept in my car and proceeded to help. Those nuts were on tight, but I was finally able to break them loose. After we got the spare on, I got back in the car and headed home. I had pulled a muscle in my right arm while straining and was wincing as I drove.

When I explained why I was hurting to Maggie, she asked the strangest question. "Why did you stop to help those people? You don't even know them." I looked at her like she was from another planet then answered the question: "Because they needed help."

Once I was hired to speak at the public library in Wausau, Wisconsin. While there I went to Walmart, and as I was leaving, found a huge roll of $20 bills on the sidewalk. I took it back in and gave to two young girls at the service desk and they couldn't believe it. But my thinking was simple – it wasn't mine and somebody will probably come back looking for it.

As I've often said: "You can take the boy from the mountain, but not the mountain from the boy."

Grit

When I was a kid, I was always looking for ways to make a buck or two. Summer jobs were easy to come by and usually pretty rough, like working the potato sheds or hauling hay. Finding ways to make money through the winter was a little tougher, but I found such a venture once via a comic book ad: selling Grit newspapers.

Do you remember that weekly paper titled Grit? I felt like a real newsboy with that white cloth bag strapped over my shoulder full of freshly printed issues. And they sold themselves. "Oh, you sell Grit?" someone would ask. "Let me get one."

And I learned early on the value of knowing your product. As soon as the new issues came out, I would read it all the way through. When someone would say they weren't interested, I would say something like, "Okay, I just thought you'd love this story in here about what this crazy lady did with kudzu." They were hooked.

What I remember most about the newspaper was all the positive stories and light-hearted humor. And they had so many comics, sometimes taking up ten full pages. I think that was the appeal to folks from areas like Sand Mountain where people are still interested in good news.

I looked up the history to learn more. It was started in 1882 by a German immigrant who established a circulation of 4000 in his first year. By the 1970s there were 30,000 newsboys like myself across rural America selling over 700,000 copies. I think I know why they were so popular. Here was the founder's motto and editorial policy:

"Always keep Grit from being pessimistic. Avoid printing those things which distort the minds of readers or make them feel at odds with the world. Avoid showing the wrong side of things, or making people feel discontented. Do nothing that will encourage fear, worry, or temptation... Wherever possible, suggest peace and good will toward men. Give our readers courage and strength for their daily tasks. Put happy thoughts, cheer, and contentment into their hearts."

When I read this I couldn't help but think what a wonderful policy this was. I also couldn't help but think that it is 180 degrees opposite of what news organizations do today. Pessimism appears to be the main trend. They seem to strive to encourage fear, worry, and discontent. And imagine a news outlet today providing happy thoughts and cheer to their audience.

Maybe we need to start up Grit newspapers again. We sure could use a news outfit today that provides good news and makes it their priority to make their readers feel good about the world. What? Peace and goodwill? Stop the presses.

City Cousins

We grew up on a small farm on Sand Mountain, but all of our cousins on our dad's side of the family lived elsewhere. Some lived in the metropolis of Fort Payne. At least it was a city in our eyes. Others lived in Georgia, North Carolina, and near Gulf Shores. We were clearly the country bumpkins of the bunch.

So when cousins came to visit us out in the sticks, we were always excited, and did what all good cousins should do: we tried to kill them. Not intentionally of course, but just by doing those things we did as kids.

I remember my cousin Garry Hulgan visiting when he was about 12 years old. We had two ponies: Pokey and Princess. Dad let Garry ride Princess and he took off up the dirt road. When he came back, however, Princess was running at top speed. I didn't even know she could move so fast. Garry seemed to be enjoying the thrill ride, until…

As she neared us, she wasn't slowing down at all. Suddenly Princess made a 90-degree left turn, but Garry didn't. He went right over her head and hit the ground and tumbled about 50 feet. He was a tad upset, but otherwise unharmed. How he walked away without breaking every bone in his body is still the mystery.

When his much younger brother, Ben Arrington, was about that same age, he had a similar experience on my little brother's minibike. He was riding very fast, and doing right well, until he wiped out. It tore his clothes up pretty good, and we picked dirt, sticks, and stones out of the cuts in his legs for a while.

If any of them spent more than a couple of hours at our place, something always seemed to happen. One stepped in a hole and sprained their ankle. One stepped on a yellow jacket nest. One was nearly decapitated walking behind the tractor when a tree snapped back. One was bitten by a hog. And the list goes on and on with cuts, bruises, and injuries galore.

I'm not sure how many times my dad had to say, "I think they're going to be okay" when their parents showed up to get them, but it was quite a few. Pretty soon the parents started making sure the kids left when they did.

I don't know if our cousins got into trouble for getting in an accident or not, but Dad was never none too happy with us for "letting" them get hurt. And I can assure you, we suffered more pain than whatever injuries they sustained.

But still, it was always fun when cousins came to visit.

Have You Ever Seen a Cat Fish?

You have? How did it hold the fishing pole? Yep, one of my dad's favorite jokes.

I can't remember the last fish I caught, but I can remember the first. I was four years old and my dad took me down to the creek and we sat on some rocks that created a five-foot ledge down to the shallow water below. I hooked a tiny mud cat and got it to the top of the rocks, but then it came off the hook.

Thank goodness my dad had fast reflexes. He grabbed one of my ankles as I went after that flopping yellow fellow as he made his way back over the edge toward the water. I wanted that fish so much that I was willing to go in after him. My love for catfish was cemented that faithful day.

I used to love taking Granny to Buddy's Pond to snag a few catfish. Owned by Buddy Wells, my uncle, it was a great place to catch a few whiskered fish and an occasional snapping turtle.

I recall one day at Hollywood, Alabama, on the Tennessee River, when I was ten years old fishing with Dad and Uncle Alden (Cotton) Wooten, so nicknamed because his hair was pure white, even as a child. They caught nothing all day but I walked away with a three-pound flathead catfish and a six-pound channel cat.

About the time I turned 12, you could add another image to our fishing spot in Hollywood. It was the nuclear power plant they began to build on the opposite bank. One day, in fact, I caught an odd fish that before that day I never knew existed. It had all the features of a catfish but instead of smooth skin, it had scales like a regular fish. Yes, a scaly catfish.

Right now you might be replaying that scene from The Simpsons where Bart caught a three-eyed fish by the nuclear power plant. But of course the plant there at Hollywood was never started, so it wasn't an apparition.

That's not to say there aren't some strange beasts in those

waters. My nephew, Van Burbol, used to go jug fishing and pull 70-pounders out of those murky waters. He hooked several even larger, but could never get those in the boat.

But the absolute crème-de-la-crème of monstrosities I've witnessed being pulled from that there river was a 210-pound shovel-bill catfish caught at the Nickajack Dam. It looked like something from another planet.

That's yet another thing I miss about the mountain — all the great catfish fishing holes. I can't wait to get back and fiddle me some worms and head to the river.

All Is Fair

This past Friday I went to the VFW Fair with my mom. It was the first time I've been to this fair in 30 years, and 25 years since I've been to any fair.

My favorite is still the art exhibits. When I was in high school I always submitted art in several different categories (and names) just to get free tickets for me and my brother and sisters. One year my pencil sketch of Ronald Reagan actually won a blue ribbon.

This year I saw many entries from artists I've gotten to know since moving back to this area two-and-a-half years ago. My nephew's wife, Emily Evans won a couple of ribbons for her photography, and my cousin, Tenice Dunn Zerbe won first place for her brownies. Congrats to those two. Just a tip: they frown upon you trying to open the display case to grab one to eat.

The food is still the hardest thing to avoid at the fair, and there are as many food vendors as there are rides. It was especially tough on me since I've been trying hard to eat right for the last month or so. Luckily it would take a small bank loan to afford a corndog and drink, so my will power prevailed. In other words, my thriftiness trumped my hunger pangs.

When I saw the Bumper Cars and Tilt-a-Whirl, I told my mom

that these were the same rides they had from when I was a kid. When she said that that's probably why they keep making them, I said, "No, I think these are the exact same rides from when I was a kid."

I noticed this year there was no regular Ferris Wheel. I always thought that was the most popular ride. They had several that resembled one, but they had cars that spun upside down instead of just normal seats that stayed upright. I guess kids today need more excitement. I remember once being at the top and thinking the people below looked like ants, until I realized it was ants on my shoe from where I had stepped in Cotton Candy.

My favorite ride was also absent – the Haunted House. Sure the Glass House is fun, but there's only so many nose bleeds you can get from walking into a glass wall before it loses its appeal. But I could ride through the Haunted House all night. After the first few times you learned where all the scary stuff was, but that mattered not; I still screamed like a five-year-old girl.

All-in-all it was a very fun evening. I saw several old classmates from Sylvania and was temporarily whisked back to my childhood.

A True Southern Thang

There are some things we know to be unique to the South, but some things are even more specific to this area of the South. Earthworms are a good example. I lived in the Montgomery area for almost 20 years, and the first time I told someone we need to fiddle some earthworms, I got blank stares. They have none in that area and they thought I was pulling their leg.

I once brought some friends home from Montgomery to show them. Convinced it was a trick like Snipe hunting, they followed me into the woods and watched as I sawed on a little hickory stump with a dull handsaw. Their smiles disappeared when those big worms started coming up through the leaves and they ran screaming from the woods.

Decoration is another great example. Since before the Civil War, it has been a yearly tradition of many in the southern Appalachian Mountains as family members "come home" from afar to gather at their family cemeteries on a specified Sunday in spring or summer to honor their dead relatives. Everyone helps to clean the cemetery, straighten old tombstones, and decorate the graves with flowers. Hence the name: Decoration.

The Dictionary of Smoky Mountain English defines Decoration as: "An occasion on which a family or a church congregation gathers … to place flowers on the graves of loved ones and to hold a memorial service for them. Traditionally this involved singing, dinner on the ground as well as a religious service."

Many historians believe that this annual recognition of the dead by Southerners was what inspired people around the country to begin honoring the fallen soldiers of the Civil War, both Union and Confederate. The practice of recognizing the Civil War dead began not long after the war ended and was observed on May 30th each year. The occasion was also known as Decoration Day.

Over the years, however, the name would change. By the end of World War II, it was commonly called Memorial Day. In 1967, the federal government made it official and changed the name to Memorial Day. It became a time to reflect on all of the servicemen from every branch of the military who died while serving.

Here in our little corner of the South, we celebrate Memorial Day with the rest of the country, but we still honor the original celebration of Decoration as well. Most of my departed family members are buried at Town Creek Cemetery in Rainsville, and today it looked like a scene from a dream. The meticulously manicured landscape was dotted with beautiful flowers of red, pink, yellow, white, purple, and blue.

You gotta love the South.

Dad the Builder

My dad was a master carpenter who wielded a framing hammer like Thor. His real gift, however, lay in knowing how to cut corners. Dad knew a magic word, and if you know this word, you'll never again need a tape measure, framing square, or level. That word is "Closeternuff." That's pronounced like its spelled: [close-ter-nuff].

I remember as a little kid holding the tools for my dad as he worked on a project. Once, when he needed a section of 2X4 to be cut a precise length, I proudly held out the tape measure. My dad smiled, shook his head and said, "I'll just eyeball it." And that's what he did. He took the circular saw and whacked off the 2X4, held it up and stared it and said, "Closeternuff."

That word guided us through a lot of home projects. I was twelve-years-old when we built the chimney for our Ashley wood-burning heater. Our system was simple: Dad would add the mortar and position the new block then I would take the level and tap it until it was perfect on all four sides.

As the chimney got higher and Dad and I were trading places up and down the ladder, Dad invoked the magic word. As I waited for him to come down so I could go up with the level, he waved me off and said "It's closeternuff. I eyeballed it."

And so it went for the rest of the way with Dad using his super vision. After that chimney was finished, Dad and I backed away to marvel at our handiwork. And wouldn't you know it; that chimney was perfectly straight — right up to where we stopped using the level. Beyond that it just sort of leaned away from the house. That didn't faze Dad. He just looked at me and said, "That'll make it draft better."

Dad was always the jokester too. When we were building our new house, we were both on the main floor in one bedroom nailing in the flooring. As I was working, I heard a nail bounce across the floor. I knew it was odd for my dad to miss, but paid no attention until it happened again, so I turned to watch.

He would hold up a handful of nails, take one and toss it aside, then hammer in another.

"Is there something wrong with some of the nails?" I asked.

Dad held up his hand displaying the nails as he had grabbed them out of the box, going in two directions. He pointed to one that was pointing upward and said, "Some of these are made to go up. I can't use them in the floor."

Coal Mine, Coal Yours

When people visit the Depot Museum, I give them a brief history of Fort Payne, explaining that it was the iron ore and coal mines that brought a lot of people here in the 1890s. I always see the curiosity in their eyes and some even ask about the coal mines.

I know what they're thinking, so I usually add that the coal mines in this area were not like the ones in West Virginia or other parts of the world. Here the coal was shallow enough that they could simply dig down to it, leaving huge open areas in the ground, or as we called them – swimming holes.

It made me remember something I had forgotten. When I was about ten years old, a man in a suit visited our little house on the backroads of Blake. He was a representative for a huge coal company and he was there with a deal, an offer to buy the mineral rights to my parents' property.

A lot of you may remember when they did this. It was a roll of the dice basically for the coal company. They paid you one payment, which gave them permission to come onto your property and drill to test for coal. If no coal was found, you kept the money. But if they found enough of it, it belonged to them and they could come in and mine for it.

Since it was all mineral rights you were selling, if they found anything like coal, silver, gold, or uranium, it belonged to them and you would never make another penny. In other words, if they paid you $500 and your property was sitting on $100 million of gold, congratulations, you were now the biggest fool on the mountain.

I watched my dad closely as the man laid out the sales pitch, my dad's dark eyes peering suspiciously out from under his thick black brows. I knew this fellow was up against a shrew negotiator and would certainly go away empty handed. As soon as his spiel was complete, my dad leaned toward him and in a stern voice said, "Where do I sign?"

The man filled out a check out for us on the spot and everyone seemed happy. A few months later the equipment came rolling in to test the ground. One hole they drilled was right beside our house, and the other was way back in the woods. Each turned up only a few inches of coal and wasn't worth the expenses to mine.

I'm pretty sure Dad breathed a sigh of relief when coal wasn't found. In fact, he probably laughed all the way to the bank.

Forgotten Skills

Growing up on Sand Mountain, there were a lot things I had to learn to do, things that I thought I would be doing for the rest of my life. But times have changed so dramatically over the last five decades, I'm sure I'll never do most of these things again.

Siphoning Gas. It seems we always needed gas back in those days for lawnmowers, cleaning parts, tractors, someone running out of gas, motorcycles, or to pour into the carburetor, etc. I was taught at a very early age how to run a cut-off garden hose down into the tank, suck on it to get the gas flowing, and run it into an old milk jug.

Since it was not an exact science, however, I usually ended up with a mouth full of gasoline. And let me tell you, that's a taste you will never forget.

Making Toys. Being on a limited budget, making our own toys was a necessary skill. I made spinning tops, kites, many flips from forked tree branches, stilts to walk on, but my favorite from memory was making a tractor from an empty wooden spool of thread using matchsticks and a rubber band

Using Ether to Inflate Tires. We always kept spray cans of ether in our cars for cold mornings when the car didn't want to start. It was super flammable and we'd spray it into the carburetor and turn the ignition. It would fire right up, usually with a bang, and the gas would keep the car running.

Another use was to help inflate tubeless tires. Since we didn't have the contraptions professional garages had to shoot a huge burst of air into the tire to seal it, we would spray ether into the tire and strike a match to it. BOOM! Tire sealed long enough to pump it up.

Making Homemade Biscuits. I used to love to do this. I'd fill a big bowl with sifted flour, pour in milk and add shortening, and slowing rake my hand around in circles as flour slowly fell off the sides to make the mix thicker and thicker. Then I'd pinch off enough to make one biscuit and roll it and pat it onto the pan. Yummy. Today I just pop open a can of Grands.

Ah there are so many things I learned growing up on the mountain, things I thought I would pass along to the younger generation. But no one siphons gas anymore, and unless I can whittle a smart phone out of a stick, no one today will care. But just wait, you little whippersnappers, when the zombie apocalypse happens, you'll wish you could make a thread spool tractor then.

Grand Central Southern Style

When I was a teenager, I read this quote from a newspaper columnist: "If you stand at Grand Central Station long enough, you'll eventually see everyone you've ever known."

I assume this is a testament to how many people go through that station. But as I've gotten older, I realize this only applies to people living in the north. I could probably stand in Grand Central Station for a year and never see anyone I know. I can't imagine any rural farmers from Sand Mountain ever needing to go there.

No, in the rural South, if you want to go somewhere that you'll eventually see everyone you've ever known, it's not a train station. "If you build it they will come" might have been made famous by the Kevin Costner movie, Field of Dreams, but it has a different meaning in the South. If you want to build something where everyone will come, build a Super Walmart.

My mom works at the Fort Payne location, and I believe she has not only seen everyone she knows, but everyone I know as well. She calls me regularly to inform me of the latest run-in with someone from my past: old friends, classmates, teachers, etc.

Mom works as a cashier and a sometimes a greeter. But the reality is we are all greeters when we go into the Super Walmart. Every time I go home to visit, I go in to see Mom, but end up seeing a lot of familiar faces. I greet them all.

I remember one time my wife and I were strolling through the store and we ran into one of my old classmates from Sylvania. It was Waylon Hall, a really great guy I hadn't seen in a coon's age. When I introduced him to Maggie as an old classmate, she looked stunned. "He's not your cousin?" she asked.

Granted, we have run into about a hundred cousins in Walmart as well. So many, in fact, that Maggie was shocked when I finally introduced her to someone who wasn't kin, at least not that I am aware.

When we do come to visit, which sadly is not even once a year, the few days I have are not enough to get around and visit with everyone I would love to see. No problem. One trip to the Super Walmart and I'm sure to catch up with some old friends and relatives.

The next class reunion we plan, we should simply ask to put up a sign at the entrance of the store. That way everyone who is still local will get the information.

So the next time I come down, I'll meet you there.

Door-to-Door

Between the ages of 11 and 13 marks the only time in my life I was a door-to-door salesman when every fall I would walk around the neighborhood selling Christmas cards. Of course everyone in our small rural area knew me and it was before you could create personalized cards with the whole family, including the pets, with any backdrop.

Things are so much different today. Besides the fact that no one trusts strangers to come to their house anymore, there are endless shopping venues in Walmartopia like Target, Kohl's, Sam's, Costco, Ebay, Amazon, and many others.

Back in the days when I sold Christmas cards, however, that wasn't the case, and some things we just expected to buy from salespeople making house calls. Our complete set of 1972 Encyclopedia Britannica with Child Craft books is a good example. That was our internet back in the day and those things saved me many times when school reports were due.

I think the giant dictionary came from the same salesman, but the large family Bible came from yet another. I was very young but I remember this fellow showing Mom and Dad that big colorful Bible full of pictures and a photo album in the back along with pages to document notable family events. And of course we would dust it off whenever the local pastors made their house calls.

I reckon most women back in those days were wooed by the traveling vacuum salesmen. Not the men themselves, but by those magical Hoover Deluxe models that could pick up even the smallest trash from your shag carpet.

Throughout our small house was yet another thing my dad bought from a door-to-door salesman: fire and smoke alarms. Unlike the small circular models of today, these were pretty large and shaped and painted like a little house. And instead of an irritating beeping sound, these things belted out a noise like a cargo ship that would wake the dead.

My dad not only bought a set of heavy duty stainless steel

cookware from a salesman who came to our house, he also signed on to be a salesman himself, and he did this successfully for many years. A lot of you older folks in the area might recall going to one of those dinners back in the day where someone cooked a dinner for you and tried to sell you a set of the cookware.

I guess it's a bygone era. Nowadays we only want service folks to come to our homes like house cleaners, lawn service crews, and even dog groomers. As for the other stuff, we'll get it the old fashioned way by ordering it online with free shipping.

Family Reunions

One good thing about being back home is I get to attend family reunions. Saturday at the Tom Bevil Center in Rainsville we held the 30th annual Wooten/Carroll reunion. I've only ever been to one of these, so it was a treat for me. And speaking of treats, oh my goodness the food…

I enjoyed seeing old cousins and remembering old times. My cousin Terry was there and we relived the story of when we were about 14 years old, walking along the creek in the dead of winter, and Terry decided to swing out over the creek on a long vine. About halfway across the vine broke and dropped him right into the icy water.

I have seen many people get frightened in my life. I've seen some people get scared out of their wits. But this was the first time I've ever witnessed someone so scared they forgot my name. Terry jumped up and down, reaching upward as he yelled, "Don't just stand there, boy. Help me, boy."

Cousin Judy was there. Once, when I was about five years old, we visited Judy and her family in South Alabama. They were showing me and my sister the empty school building near their home when a car drove by. Judy convinced us we were in trouble because driving the car was the invisible man who owned the school, and hated visitors.

As I've mentioned before, you'll be hard pressed to find someone more gullible than I. Our only hope was for one of us to make it across this long ditch and back to Judy's house. Her brother tried but the invisible man caught him and almost killed him. He barely made it back to the school and conveyed this message: "He said if we tried again, he would kill us."

That's when Judy looked at me and said, "Okay, Neal, it's your turn." To which I'm sure I responded with something like, "I'm sorry. Say what?" Of course I can't be too upset with Judy's prank since later that week she saved my life. I was choking on a dime and she whacked me in the back and dislodged it.

Cousin Karen brought me several pictures from her mom's collection including several of me and my older sisters when we were very young and one of my dad when he was in the Army, a picture I had never seen before.

The entire day was a blast. The center was filled to capacity with cousins, aunts, uncles, and enough food to feed the entire student body at Northeast Alabama Community College. I think the invisible man might also have been there, but I didn't see him.

Back in My Day

As I've gotten older, I have inadvertently turned into my dad. Everything from my youth was better than it is today – the music, the movies, the food, etc. I'm not sure if things really were better when I was growing up or if it's simply that human trait called pride. You know: "mine is better than yours."

But my dad was the same way. When I was young, he was always comparing the things of that day to things from his own upbringing, and the things from his time were always better.

For example, Dad loved Jersey milk. There was a man who lived over by Winkles Groceries who had a Jersey cow and sold milk in those large one-gallon canning jars. I hated it. It tasted like grass to me. I much preferred the store-bought milk, but Dad loved it.

We actually had a churn at one point so we could make butter the old fashioned way just for Dad. Sure, we could have gone to the store and bought a huge tub for one dollar, but it didn't compare in Dad's eyes, so my sisters and I spent about ten hour churning milk into butter. And it was horrible to me.

That wasn't the only thing we used the churn for. Dad also used to make Home Brew. Have you heard of this? It's not quite like moonshine, but based on the same principle. It had a taste somewhere between castor oil and battery acid, but to Dad it was better than a six pack of Bud.

Then there was the time Dad wanted to start making sorghum syrup the old fashioned way. We even planted about ten acres of sugarcane. Luckily by the time the cane matured, Dad had already lost interest, so we never did build the mill with all that antique equipment. Whew!

Home remedies always worked better than over-the-counter drugs too, at least according to my dad. He never bought Alka Seltzer. He swore by his glass of water and vinegar mixed with baking soda concoction. His home treatments for bee stings and toothaches were better, as well as for coughs, callouses, cramps, cuts, and constipation.

Dad despised canned biscuits, was appalled by TV Dinners, and hated instant grits, instant oatmeal, instant coffee, instant everything. He thought rock-n-roll music should be outlawed, microwaves should be banned, and every black-and-white movie ever made was better than any garbage that hit the big screen lately.

Like I said, I guess it's just human nature. So just think, in 40 years the youth of today will be defending all the stuff from their childhood to the kids of tomorrow.

Do You Remember These?

Things from DeKalb County stick in my memory, just simple images most times, but these images stay forever. See how many you remember.

Do you remember the first video arcade in Fort Payne named The Silver Ball Arcade? But going back further, do you remember when there was a go cart racetrack right off main street in Fort Payne? Or going back even further, how about the miniature golf course also right off main street?

Do you remember when Herbert Mitchell used to spray water on his yard and trees ever year during the holidays to create a winter wonderland? If you go back even further, do you remember when he ran for Constable on Fort Payne and upset all the normal law enforcement agencies? And going way way back, do you remember when he ran a produce stand at the South Y and collected empty milk jugs, which he stored in cotton trailers?

Do you remember Jenny's Drive-in in Fort Payne? Do you remember when there was a drive-in restaurant about halfway through town? Do you remember when Jack's served the best burgers (the Bonanza Burger) anywhere around? By the way, you can still get those at The Strand.

Do you remember Finley's groceries in Sylvania? Do you remember Mrs. Finely giving her football predictions? Do you remember when the town hall and post office shared a building next door? Or going way back, do you remember a drive-in theater in Sylvania?

Most people remember when headlight dimmer switches on cars were positioned on the floor to the left of the brake pedal. But did you ever own a car or truck that had the starter button there? We did. And we also owned a tractor that had the spin rod in the front to crank the motor.

Do you remember when the Walmart in Fort Payne was in the building across from McDonalds? But do you remember the business that was there before Walmart? It was called Big K. Do you remember Bargain Town or all the five and ten cent stores?

Do you remember when there was a Sarah Lee Bakery in Fort Payne? Do you remember when it was called Merico? Do you remember when there was a bakery outlet at what used to be the first red-light coming from the North Y? Do you remember Hurley's Market across the street?

Do you remember when doctors made house calls? Okay, that was a little before my time. But I do remember when preachers made house calls. Do you remember all the dirt roads and wobbly wooden bridges on the mountain? Do you remember being happy to see the road graders come?

These are some things I remember.

Family TV Time

I remember as a kid growing up on Sand Mountain, we owned one of those state-of-the-art 25-inch color console televisions with the wooden cabinet and built in speakers on each side of the screen. Someone had given it to us already broken and when we could never get it to work it became the stand for our 19-inch TV.

That TV had two plastic knobs, the top for VHF and the bottom for UHF. I can still hear my dad telling us not to turn the knobs too fast or they would break. I knew he was just being paranoid. Of course it turned out he was right and we used pliers for many years to change the channels.

We only had a VHF antenna, which means we could get channels 3, 9, and 12 out of Chattanooga. Remember those windy days when the picture would get fuzzy and your dad would send you out to the antenna? "OK, turn it. It's getting better. A little more. No, go back. That's it; don't move."

Still the television was the apex of technology, and it served as the center of nightly family events. The kids may have been the remote controls, but Mom and Dad were the ones who picked the programs to watch. But they did a great job. We always watched Gun Smoke, Gilligan's Island, The Brady Bunch, Hee Haw, and a host of other family-friendly shows.

I always stayed up late on weekends and during the summer, usually falling asleep and waking when I heard the National Anthem being played and I would see the American Flag on the TV screen and hear them say, "This concludes another day of broadcasting."

I would turn it to channel 19 out of Huntsville since we could then get the signal and it was clear enough to watch. And, occasionally, it would be a Tarzan movie, and when that happened, all was right with the world. I could forget any other worries when the Lord of the Jungle, Jane, Cheetah, and Boy were doing their thing.

Now I have a 50-inch flat plasma TV mounted to the wall in my den and get over 300 channels and hardly watch anything anymore. How did television get so much more advanced, yet still lose its magic? Is it because we have so many other technological devices to distract us? Or is it having so many channels to choose from that makes it not special?

Like growing up when Mom would very rarely buy ice cream and it was awesome. I guess if we had it all the time, it wouldn't have meant as much. But dog gone it, I was willing to take that chance.

Have You Ever

Going back to the mountain for a visit always fires up my memory. But things have changed so much since I grew up there. I don't think I saw one dirt road when I was home. Even my mom's road is now graveled. I realize there are a lot of things that I did when I was a kid that I'll probably never get to do again. How many have you done?

Have you ever picked Poke Salad or smoked a cigarette made from Rabbit Tobacco? Have you ever made a corncob pipe? Have you ever canned wild blackberries or make Muscadine wine? Have you ever sucked the nectar from a Honeysuckle or chewed on the bark from a maple tree?

Have you ever split firewood, used an outhouse, or crafted a wooden rabbit trap? Have you ever made a slingshot from a forked stick and old inner tube, or made a toy tractor out of a rubber band and empty thread spool?

Have you ever gone inside the Hole-in-the-Rock, toured Sequoyah Caverns, explored the caves at Ider or on Pine Ridge, camped out all night in a cemetery, or took a midnight ride through Bobo Hollow?

Have you ever watched Shock Theater, watched a movie from the balcony of the DeKalb Theatre, or filled a bread bag with popcorn to go to the drive-in? Have you ever had to turn the antenna or fell asleep on the couch when the networks went off the air?

Have you ever stayed barefoot all day, played Flies and Skinners, Mumbly Peg, Red Rover, Freeze Tag, Hide and Seek, Kick the Can and Run and Hide, Ring Around the Rosies, Drop the Handkerchief, Mother May I, One-Two-Three Red Light, or Hopscotch?

Have you ever swam in the creek or the coal mines, spent all night on the Tennessee River or Weiss Lake, caught a snapping turtle, fiddled earthworms, hiked Little River Canyon, gone frog gigging, or nailed a catfish to a tree to skin it?

Have you ever put a June bug on a string, put a wad of tobacco on a bee sting, caught lightning bugs, fought pincher bugs, or stepped in a fire ant bed?

Have you ever worked at a potato shed, played on the caboose at the city park, cut down your own Christmas tree, made your own Christmas tree decorations, or rolled someone's yard?

Aww, to be a kid again on Sand Mountain. Looking back, I'm not sure how we stayed outside and played all day during the summer. Was it cooler then or were we simply tougher? Maybe a little of both. But these are some things that will forever linger in my memory.

Ghost of Christmas Past

A lot of people complain about the commercialization of Christmas, and I am old enough to have seen a lot of changes since I was a kid. The megastore super sales and all the latest high tech gizmos are nothing like the Christmases I grew up with on the mountain.

One of my fondest memories was getting our Christmas tree. We had never heard of Christmas tree farms and had certainly never entertained the idea of buying an artificial tree. So from the time I was about eight years old, I'd accompany my dad every year deep into the woods looking for the best tree we could find.

Our property didn't have spruces or Douglas Firs, or anything fancy like that, so we would try to find the best possible regular old pine tree to cut down, one that hopefully had only one bald spot that we could turn toward the wall. We'd cut it down and drag it all the way back to the house.

Remember those old stands that had a metal ring to slide the tree into with three bolts to tighten against the trunk? There was a red bowl underneath to add water. By today's standards, our trees were awfully bare, but it's all we knew back then and putting that tree up was a wonderful family affair.

Mom always made popcorn and gave us a needle with a long thread so we could make popcorn string decorations. And we had that one sting of Christmas tree lights that took us an hour to unravel every year. It was comprised of large red, blue, green, and orange lights that didn't flash, twinkle, or do anything special, but once lit, it still mesmerized me and my sisters.

Trying to get to sleep that night was an exercise in torture, but in the wee hours of the morning, slumber finally came. Then, around 5:00 every Christmas morning, my oldest sister would wake us all up to let us know Santa had come. I can't even describe that feeling and there's never been anything else like it in life.

We knew Mom and Dad would be sleeping late, although I never knew why, but seeing those wrapped presents under the tree was the epitome of anticipation. Our presents were never the latest high tech toys, and certainly not the most expensive, but that didn't matter. It was still magical.

Everything that day was always perfect, from the presents and my mom's homemade Christmas treats, to visiting friends and relatives throughout the day. Even with the newfangled trees, lights, and commercialization of Christmas, I hope kids everywhere still feel the way I did on Christmas morning.

Merry Christmas.

It's a Sand Mountain Thing

We had a family cookout on Saturday and my mom reminded me that Sunday was Decoration at the cemetery where my grandfather is buried. I remember growing up thinking this was a national event, but it turns out to be much more localized. In fact, I think this long-standing tradition might just be in this small corner of the rural south.

I know they never heard of it across the Georgia line or in Montgomery either. Another thing they never heard of in Montgomery is a Rick of wood. They knew the common size referred to as a Cord, but a Rick, which is basically the same length as a Cord, but only one stack of cut wood wide, was not a part of their units of measure.

Once, while discussing an up-and-coming fishing trip with a friend in Montgomery, I asked where a good place might be to fiddle for earthworms. My friend looked at me like I was speaking a foreign language. She had never heard of such, and did not believe me when I explained the size of earthworms.

This called for a road trip to Sand Mountain to prove I wasn't pulling her leg. I drove to my parents' home and grabbed an old handsaw and headed into the woods. My friend hesitated. "Wait a minute," she said. "Is this like Snipe hunting? Are you going to take me deep into the woods and leave me?"

Gee, I wish I had thought of that. I finally convinced her to venture a few feet into the woods where she could still see the house, and cut down a small hardwood and began to saw across the top to create the needed vibrations. When she started screaming, I knew it was working as foot-long earthworms began crawling on top of the leaves.

Sand Mountain is truly a unique place to grow up with many peculiarities that are strictly our own. Sure they have Mardi Gras in new Orleans, but we have the Potato Festival right here in Henagar. They might have Comic Con in Atlanta, but we have UFO Days right here in Fyffe.

It's good to be back home where I can pay my respects to the dearly departed on a special day, fiddle me some earthworms and catch a mess of catfish, cook them over some hickory from my Rick of wood, and drink a nice cold glass of sweet tea since it's still a dry county.

By the way, the term "sweet tea" even confuses people up north and out west, and when I would tell people I'm from a dry county, they would look confused and ask, "Are you guys having a drought?"

Sand Mountain Critters

I still have my first-grade report card. There's a note at the bottom from my teacher, Delight Garmany. It reads: "Neal is a wonderful student except for an occasional snake."

It took me many years to realize that my mom and my teachers didn't share my love of reptiles, although I still don't understand it. By the time I was ten, my mom would make me empty my pockets before she would let me in the house.

That's one thing I miss from Alabama—the snakes and other

such varmints. And growing up on Sand Mountain, I've seen my share of crazy critters.

I've seen stray cats, wildcats, bobcats, and polecats. I've seen corn snakes, king snakes, black racers, hog nosed snakes, copperheads, water moccasins, and rattlers. I've seen more possums than you can shake a stick at. Warning: do not shake sticks at possums.

I once saw a groundhog the size of a six-year-old kid. It was sitting on our wood pile one winter as if it owned the property. And yes, it did make me wonder how much wood could a woodchuck chuck if a woodchuck could chuck wood.

One day, at the Tennessee River, I saw a 210-pound shovelbill (or spoonbill) catfish brought out of the water. That same day, I caught a five-pound scaly catfish. I first thought it had something to do with the fact that we were in Hollywood fishing by the giant nuclear reactors, but this wasn't like the three-eyed fish Bart Simpson caught. It turns out that catfish with scales really do exist.

I saw a blue owl once that was so large and scary it looked like it could carry off a Shetland pony. I've seen grey squirrels, brown squirrels, red squirrels, and even a flying squirrel. I once saw a mermaid in the creek. (I made that one up to see if you were still paying attention.)

One night, when I was about 12 years old, I realized something was sleeping with me. It was a cold winter night and I could feel it pressed up against my lower leg. It was about the size of a cat, which would have made me feel better if we had actually owned a cat. Whatever it was, I decided it just needed the warmth, so I never raised the blankets to look. Well, that and I was scared out of my wits. In the morning, it was gone.

But the way I figure it is, we're all on God's green earth together, so let's make the best of it. With all the cities expanding and the forests being destroyed in favor of new constructions, I'm glad to know that there are still places on the mountain for critters to thrive.

Up here, most of the critters I see have two legs, two arms, one cell phone, and can't decide which lane they want to stay in on the expressway.

Magic on the Mountain

I don't believe in Bigfoot, aliens from outer space, vampires, werewolves, or anything supernatural. However, growing up on Sand Mountain, I've witnessed my share of Southern superpowers that I can't explain.

Julene, my oldest sister, could take warts away. People would come from all around the area just to get her to do this. How did she do it? She bought them. She would pay the person a nickel or dime for the wart, and a few days later it would be gone. I have no idea how or why that worked.

When I was young, we still had a medicine man in our community. It was a person who knew all the home remedies and could cure anything from Whooping Cough to Yellow Jaundice. This knowledge and ability was passed down through each generation alternating from male to female.

Bee charmers are people who can stroll right up to wild honeybee nests, reach their hand in and bring out a huge honeycomb dripping with fresh honey, then walk away unscathed. I can't even get within 20 feet of a nest without getting stung.

I've seen several water witches in action. It used to be that whenever someone built a new house, or just needed a well dug, they hired a water witch to find the best location to dig. Usually utilizing a forked stick from a willow or sassafras tree, the water witch walks around the property until the forked stick is pulled toward the earth by an invisible force.

This might seem unbelievable, but I'll bet you can find people on the mountain who can vouch for the success. In fact, I'm guessing water witches are still used today.

I knew a woman who had several wells dug and each produced iron water, which caused her hair to be a reddish-orange. Her neighbor across the road had clear water, so she hired a water witch to trace the same spring her neighbor used. It worked. He followed it across to her property and told them where to dig, and ta-dah — clear water.

I once went to a Holiness church in Mentone that used rattlesnakes. They had a congregation of about 20 people and pulled out a box of six rattlesnakes and started passing them around. They offered me one but I realized there wasn't enough to go around and I don't have a greedy bone in my body. But no one got bit.

My granddad Pete Wooten could run faster and jump higher than most mortals. I used to believe that my cousin J.W. had canine DNA because he could find more rabbits that the beagles. That's Sand Mountain. I bet you know a few people with strange powers too.

Shake On It

Dad was selling an old farm truck for $800. I was 12 years old and I witnessed the transaction between him and another local farmer, but the money that changed hands didn't appear right. After the farmer shook my dad's hand, he drove away in the truck.

I had to ask. "How much did he pay you?"

"Two hundred dollars," Dad answered.

"Is that all?"

"That's all he had," Dad replied. "He'll pay me the rest."

"How can you be sure?" I asked.

Dad looked at me like I was crazy. "Because he shook on it."

Dad was right. The farmer did pay the rest as soon as he had it. It wasn't because he had money to spare nor was it because he knew the truck was worth it. It was because of the reason Dad said – he shook on it.

Back in that day in this country, or at least in the rural South, contracts meant nothing. Signatures meant little more. But to shake a man's hand and tell him you're going to do something was giving your word, and that held more weight than any paper ever could.

A man might not have much money or belongings in this world, but what every man had was his image, his sense of worth, and that meant something. Keeping your word was a matter of respect, of honesty, integrity, and honor. It was the one true value for which you could measure another.

And it wasn't enough just to shake a man's hand, you had to do it right. The first time I shook my dad's hand he frowned and shook his head. "No, no," he said. "Don't hand me a dead fish. When you shake a man's hand, you look him in the eye and grab his hand firmly and squeeze. Let him know you mean it."

These lessons have resonated with me throughout my life, lessons that have almost disappeared with my Dad's generation. I am reminded of this every time I shake the hand of a younger fellow and receive the dead-fish treatment. There's no connection, no bond, just what probably seems to them as a silly gesture.

It might even seem silly to you. But to me it's a reflection of our entire society. If boys today are not taught the value of something as simple as shaking another man's hand, how then will they ever understand the importance of every positive trait a man should have that is conveyed through this action?

As for me, I'll just continue the way I was taught. So if we meet or do business together, be prepared to shake my hand and possibly wince in pain when I squeeze.

Maternal Words of Wisdom

It's no secret that Southern moms possess the ultimate words of enlightenment, and often bombard their children with the valuable tidbits of wisdom that shame even the likes of Plato, Aristotle, and Socrates.

"If your friends jumped off a bridge, would you do it, too?" That was a tough one. I needed more information to make a judgment call on that one. How high was the bridge? Was it over water or a highway? Was there a pretty girl involved?

My mom used to tell me and my sister, "If you're going to play on the couch, get in the floor." After we pondered the meaning of that cryptic verse for a while, we'd already forgotten what we were playing to begin with.

"Stop crying or I'll give you something to cry about." That was more than a little confusing. Obviously I already had something to cry about or I wouldn't be crying. But it takes a caring mom to make sure you're crying for the right reasons.

The most confusing thing my mom used to say to me, however, was whenever we were about to go somewhere in the car. She would say, "Make sure you have on clean underwear. What if we're in an accident?"

I wasn't really clear on what the status of my underwear had to do with anything, so I asked her. She explained. "If I have a wreck and we have to be taken to the hospital, you'll want to have on clean underwear."

I said, "Mom, if you have a wreck, I'm pretty sure I'm going to soil my underwear." Heck, her normal driving scared the crap out of me. But she had me worried. I could see the doctors in the ER refusing to give me mouth-to-mouth because of the lump in the back of my jeans.

Other wonderful Momisms are:

"Money doesn't grow on trees, You'll put an eye out, Your face will freeze that way, Be careful what you wish for, That is why we can't have nice things, If I've told you once; I've told you a thousand times, Just wait until your father gets home, You'd lose your head if it wasn't attached, Kids in Africa would be happy to have what you have, Because I said so; that's why, and Were you born in a barn?"

And of course the ultimate motherly smack down when all else failed: "When you grow up, I hope you have kids that act just like you!"

Keeping Time Southern Style

We all know the standard measures of time: seconds, minutes, hours, days, weeks, months, years, and so on. But not every event falls into such organized quantum units. Hence we Southerners have developed a more personal form of communication regarding the passage of time.

Fixin' to: This is the shortest frame of time in the Southern language. It means immediately. If you say you're fixin' to do something, then you're going to begin upon finishing the sentence. Or if your mom says you're fixin' to get a whooping if you don't stop making noise, well the time to stop is right now because you're out of time.

Two Shakes of a Cow's Tail: This phrase was borrowed from the phrase "Two Shakes of a Lamb's Tail." But since we have few sheep herders on the mountain and tons of cattle pastures, it just fit better. It's a very short period of time as you might suspect. My dad used it a lot playing checkers. "This game will be over in two shakes of a cow's tail," he would say then jump every piece I had on the board.

A Jiffy: This is also a very brief span. We use this to express to others that whatever it is we have to do will be over quickly. If you go to the counter of a convenience store and the clerk says he will be with you in a jiffy; that means a matter of seconds or minutes, just as soon as he stops texting his girlfriend.

Directly (Often pronounced Dreckly): The meaning of this particular expression varies and is subjective to the event it references. If you tell someone you're going to the bathroom and will be back directly, it could mean a few minutes. If you say you're going to the state line to buy lottery tickets and will be back directly, it could mean hours. It simply means you're going directly there, do your business, and come directly back.

A Month of Sundays: This is a longer period of time.

Technically it means about 30 Sundays or 30 weeks. If someone says they haven't been to church in a month of Sundays, it means more than half a year but not quite a year. It also means they have to hide from the pastor whenever they see him in public.

A Coon's Age: This can be quite a few years. It was believed long ago that raccoons lived very long lives, so this term became associated with that belief. If someone tells you they haven't seen you in a coon's age, it means that it's been many years.

How many of these do you use?

Southern Hospitality

We've all heard that phrase, but is that really all it is anymore? Times have changed so much, I wonder if Southern Hospitality still exist or is just a term from a bygone era.

There was a time that I would never pass a stranded motorist. I would always stop to see if I could be of assistance, either with my limited mechanic skills or just to provide a ride. Now-a-days everyone has a cell phone and has already called a family member or AAA, and stare at you funny if you stop to help.

In the last 20 years, I have been to the home of friends or acquaintances where other people in the home never acknowledged my presence. Once it was a coworker and we sat in the den watching TV. His wife came into the room twice and never looked at me or said anything and he never introduced us. That was so weird to me.

My dad was perhaps the meanest cuss this side of the Tennessee River, but if you were in his home, you were given the royal treatment. He spoke to you with a genuine interest, told you several jokes from his unlimited reservoir, and more than once would offer to feed you.

Once I came up from Montgomery with three friends from my gym because they wanted to compete at a powerlifting meet in Scottsboro. I never told Dad we were coming, or that I was bringing three friends, all of whom were African American.

It didn't matter. Dad greeted them in the usual Southern manner. We rode down to Scottsboro for the weigh-in and when we got back, Dad had cooked them all breakfast. And as I've mentioned, Dad's breakfasts were legendary. From the looks on my friends' faces, they had never seen anything like it.

After we ate, Dad came along to the weight-lifting event and cheered them on. My friends couldn't get over how well my dad treated them, thinking he was the nicest guy on the planet. But the fact is, they were guests, and that's just what you're supposed to do.

Another memory I have from when I was young, is sometimes at suppertime, Dad would decide we needed to visit some relatives. We'd all pile in the car and go visit some kin folks who were also getting ready for supper. They'd greet us cheerfully and add chairs and plates to the table. Sometimes we would have relatives show up unannounced for supper too. It was considered an honor.

Imagine doing that today. A carload of relatives showing up would probably scare the crap out of me. And I seriously doubt I'd have enough chicken nuggets to go around.

Fake Monster News

Back during Halloween I mentioned how much I enjoy hearing old timers spin yarns about monsters, but stories of fake monsters are just as entertaining.

My dad used to tell about a time when he and his cousin were fishing at Chisenhall Spring. It was nearing midnight and Dad wanted to go home, but his cousin wanted to stay, so Dad came up with a plan. "Did you hear that?" Dad said suddenly and spun around to look into the woods. His cousin shook his head, but began to get worried. "I heard something behind us in the trees," Dad added. "There it was again."

"I heard it that time," his cousin said. It's amazing how easy it is to trick the mind. Obviously there was no sound, but now his cousin was paying more attention to the woods than his fishing pole. Finally he returned his focus to fishing.

Dad took a stick and tossed it into the trees behind them. When it landed, his cousin jumped up and ran up the little dirt trail and back to the car as fast as he could go. Dad gathered all the fishing equipment and followed. When he got to the car he asked his cousin if he heard it again and he replied, "Heard it nothing. I saw it."

A few days ago I was talking with Bobby Fortner. Y'all might remember Mr. Fortner from years past when he owned Easy Curb beside Beason's Barber Shop in Fort Payne. When I was a kid we always stopped in there to get a big bag of that crushed ice to take to the lake. But Mr. Fortner grew up on Sand Mountain near where I did, and even went to Blake school for several years.

He told me of a time when he was a little kid, not even in his teens. He and several other boys were walking home from church one night. There were dark clouds covering a moonless sky, so it was basically pitch black. The older boys took off running and left him behind.

Not wanting to be alone, little Bobby took off running too. And that's when he heard it. Something was following him. He could hear the rhythm of it closing in on him. He ran faster but the mysterious creature kept up with him. Finally his lungs were heaving and he had to slow down. The creature slowed down too.

No matter what pace he ran, this thing in the dark matched his speed exactly. And then, there on that dark road, the horror became clear. His corduroy pants were rubbing together at his thighs while he ran.

I couldn't stop laughing.

Tricks of the Hillbilly Trade

Growing up in the rural South back in the 70s, you learned a lot of tricks for getting things done. For example, before fuel injection, most people kept a spray can of ethyl in their cars. If the car wouldn't start due to cold weather or old gas, you could spray the ethyl right into the carburetor and, being more flammable than gas, would help get it going.

Another use for ethyl was in helping to inflate flat tires. If a tubeless tire had lost its seal, you couldn't simply add air. Service stations use a machine that blows a blast of air into the tire to seal it. But normal folks didn't own such, so you could spray ethyl into the tire, light it causing it to explode and the tire to seal, allowing you to pump it up.

If you had a snapping turtle in your pond and couldn't catch him with a fishing pole, here's a way to do it. Take a long board about a foot wide and attach fishing hooks with screws to the board. Place them so the points are facing the top, where you add a piece of meat. The turtle will crawl up the board over the hooks, but can't crawl back down. He'll be there waiting for you in the morning.

If you need a mess of crawfish for your Jambalaya, it's an easy thing to accomplish. Take as many soup cans as you can find, make a small hole in the top edge and tie a string to it, and drop them in the creek. Go back the next morning and every can will have a large crawfish. It works every time.

Once we had a young boar that weighed about a hundred pounds. Dad decided he needed to be castrated. The hog didn't think so, and even three grown men couldn't hold him. Then someone told me the way to do it. We filled the bottom of a 55-gallon drum with feed, turned it on its side, and when the hog went into it to eat, we simply turned the drum upright. The young boar was on its nose with his legs spread wide, and he couldn't move.

Now-a-days most 55-gallon drums are made of plastic, but you can still find the old metal ones around the South. That's because of another trick that a lot of old timers used. Fill the drum with water and corn. After the corn rots, light a fire under the drum. Keep the temperature of the water between 180 and 212 degrees. Run a copper tube in circles out of the top to cool the steam being produced. Catch the drops into a jug. Drink. Repeat. (Warning – also more flammable than gas.)

My Old Man

I have always considered myself above average in certain areas: strength, coordination, and possibly even smarts. But one sad truth I have to admit to is that my dad was better than me at, well… everything.

You did not want to play checkers with this man. I never won one game against him my entire life. When you see those old timers sitting around the small stores and city park playing checkers, trust me, it's not just a game, it's a calculated strategic event. Dad always told me to look four moves ahead, but I was lucky to know where my next piece was going.

And forget throwing horseshoes. Like most people, I tried to make the shoe flip one time in air and hopefully land around the stake. But Dad held the horseshoe on the side and made it rotate 360 degrees instead of flipping it. And if it landed anywhere near the stake, it slid right around it. I once watched him win ten games in a row and threw a ringer every time.

My senior year in high school, I was the fastest lineman on the football team, running the 40 in under five seconds. Had God seen fit to bless me with normal length legs instead of these stubby things, there's no telling how fast I could have been. Yet my dad, who was 47 at the time and horribly out of shape, could smoke me. In fact, Dad could run backward with me running forward and still outrun me.

Between the ages of 18 and 25, I racked up dozens of arm wrestling and powerlifting trophies. I hit the gym religiously. Yet Dad, who had never stepped foot in a fitness center in his life, could toss me around like a rag doll and beat me at arm wrestling easily.

To make matters worse, it wasn't just physical things he excelled at. I was on the math team in high school and once even won a first place trophy for that. Dad, however, who never made it past elementary school, was even sharper. He could do advanced mathematics in his head faster than most people can do them on a calculator.

I've always read that to get better at something, you need to compete with those better than you. Well, that sums up my entire life with regards to my dad. I truly think it was a great thing having a father so capable. That might be why I did do well in certain areas, just from the competition.

There's actually a verse in the Bible that explains it better. Proverbs 27:17 (NIV) says, "As iron sharpens iron, so one person sharpens another."

Henagar, Alabama

Admittedly, when I was a kid going to school at Sylvania, I didn't know a lot about our neighbor to the north. It was just this place from where we picked up a bunch of new students in the 9th grade. Oh, and I also know I spelled it wrong almost every time I wrote it.

It turns out there's a reason for that. I was spelling it correctly and it is the town that spells it the wrong way. Doing a little research and I learned it was named after George Henegar. When the post office was built in 1878, however, a postal official misspelled the town's name as "Henagar." I guess you could say the whole town went postal.

What I can tell you about the town today is that it's one of my favorite places. A couple of years ago, after my novel about Granny Dollar was released, I was contacted by the librarian at Henagar Library about doing a book-signing. I've done enough of these events in small towns to realize the chance of selling more than a few books is slim at best.

Boy was I wrong. I got there 15 minutes early and someone rushed out to my car to see if I could hurry because there was already a line of people waiting. It was like that the entire time I was there and I met so many wonderful folks and sold about 60 books. Subsequent book-signings have proven great as well.

And let's not forget the drive-in theater. I'm from that generation that still remembers drive-ins fondly. I went to the Hamilton in Fort Payne many times. When I go to the movies at the one in Henagar, I am instantly whisked back to my childhood and it's great.

The PrattMont Theater between Montgomery and Prattville was still in operation when I moved to that area in 1987. I went once and it was raining and I got drenched from hanging that huge speaker in the window. I remember thinking, "Why don't they broadcast the sound over the radio?" Apparently I was ahead of my time.

And the Potato Festival is just plain fun. I had some friends up visiting last year on the Fourth weekend, and their daughter, Tatyana, is an up-and-coming singer. I took them to the festival and we asked the events coordinator if she could sing a few songs, and even though they had a full schedule, they were so polite and worked her in. And the crowd response was awesome.

Throw all that together with great residents, great shops, and great restaurants, and you got a place that is the true epitome of Southern hospitality.

Coaches

By now you've probably seen the video of the two high school football players from Texas blindsiding an official. First they claimed it was because he made racial slurs, but now they're saying their assistant coach ordered them to do it because he had made bad calls.

Whatever the reason, it is more evidence of how things have changed. I can't imagine this happening when I was in school. Coaches were tough and fearsome for sure, but they taught players respect above all else, respect for your team, your opponents, and certainly officials. If a ref made a bad call, the coach took it up with the ref himself.

Coaches in small rural towns are more than coaches. Sure, they have to teach classes as well, but that's not what I mean. Coaches not only taught you the game, they were like father figures who taught you about integrity, winning, losing, teamwork, humility, and life in general.

When I was 12 my mom drove me to a potato shed where I hoped to get a summer job. It was owned by my basketball coach, Clinton Graham. He didn't have a job but he told my mom to go on home. He personally drove me to other sheds and vouched for me until someone hired me. I'll never forget that. But coaches looked out for their players and for all students.

My junior high football coach, Johnny Edwards, was the epitome of a football coach. He was strong, loud, tough, and relentless. He loved to grab you by the facemask and shake you like a ragdoll. Next to my dad, I think he was the scariest person I've ever known. And we loved him. Because no matter how overbearing he seemed, everything he did was done out of a genuine caring to make us not just better players, but better human beings.

My first varsity coach was William Drinkard. Maybe coaching was not his forte since we only won one game in the three years he was at Sylvania. But he was a still a man of character. I remember once helping him chalk the field and he relentlessly asked me about my grades and my plans after school.

Coach Thomas replaced him and like all my former coaches, was all about getting you to do better at everything, not just football. There was an authentic caring about him.

You probably have fond memories of a coach who helped you find your better self. It might not even be something we think about but something deep inside our subconscious that guides us. Chances are, if you have determination and the will to succeed, there's a coach or teacher somewhere behind it.

Sure, We Had That

Often we talk about how far we've come in the last few decades in regards to technology, but looking back I realize we had a lot of the same things when I was younger that we have now. Instead of it being electronic devices, however, it was called "Kids."

Mom sent messages all the time. But instead of texting on a cell phone, she used me or my sisters. We would deliver messages like "Mom said come eat" to each member of the family individually to places like the living room, bedrooms, yard, or woods. If we didn't come right away, the next message would come from Dad, and we never ignored that one.

And yes, of course we had a dishwasher. It was the kids again. My sisters and I rotated each night in two-person teams, one to wash and one to rinse.

We definitely had voice messaging. Anytime someone called for Mom or Dad, we used our voice to give them the message when they got home. "Uncle Bob called. He and Aunt Helen and their 12 kids are coming for supper tonight."

A remote control you ask? You better believe it. That was us again. Dad didn't even have to get out of his chair. He'd just point and one of us would hop up and change the channel. This was usually followed by him saying, "Don't turn it so fast or you'll break the knob."

Do you know that televisions today have built-in tracking devices to ensure that the strongest signal is received? Yep, we had that too. It was the kids again sent outside to turn the antenna. "Stop! No, go back. That's it. Don't move!"

The Internet is a great source for information and we had that too. It was in hardcover format on the bookshelves and called Encyclopedias. We just had to surf the pages until we found what we were looking for.

Just like now, we had tons of gaming choices. But of course we didn't sit in front of a TV or computer like kids today. We literally played gamed like Hide-and-Seek, Flies-and-Skinners, Kick the Can and Run and Hide, Ring Around the Roses, Hopscotch, and a lot more.

We even had GPS. That was me. Anytime we went someplace new, I was the one who rode shotgun with the huge map and gave Dad directions. I can still remember how his face looked when I would say something like, "Uh, that road we just passed. That's where we should have turned."

When I think about it, most of the high-tech gizmos today are things that make life easier for kids. No wonder they have so much time to devote to texting and video games.

Frog

In keeping with stories from my school days at Sylvania, here's another. It involves one of the most likeable teachers I ever had – Billy Jack Lee. How cool a name is that? It's like a cross between Billy Jack and Bruce Lee. Of course our teacher, Mr. Lee, resembled neither, and I seriously doubt he was a master of martial arts.

He got his nickname, Frog, because he always sat on top of his desk during class with his legs crossed and he had particularly loose neck skin. This moniker was strictly in admiration because we all loved the guy. I don't remember actually learning any school stuff from him, but I sure learned a lot about life.

But he, like a lot of teachers from that era, was a no-nonsense type of person. He fully believed in discipline and could dish it out with the best of them, even if you were innocent. When students would say, "It's not fair," Mr. Lee would simply smile and counter with, "It doesn't have to be fair; it can be cloudy outside." Seriously, who can argue with that logic?

As for myself, well, I was never innocent, and I felt the brunt of Mr. Lee's paddle many times. Even his paddle was unique. Unlike other teachers' paddles, which were broad and thin, his was only about 2.5 inches across and a full 1.5 inches thick, and he could wield it like Babe Ruth. And it was green. I know – what other color could Frog's paddle be? And it hurt something awful.

One day another student and I decided tough times called for tough measures and we stole Mr. Lee's paddle. We figured it was for the good of the entire student body. I won't say who the other student was, but he lives at the top of the mountain and owns a business called Terry Summerford Taxidermy.

So me and this other student, we'll call him…uh, Terry I guess, took the paddle to the back of the gym, leaned it against the block wall, and jumped up and down on it to break it. It wouldn't break. It didn't even splinter.

Concluding that it was made of a material not from this world, we took it back to Mr. Lee and confessed to what we had done, or at least what we had tried to do. He roared with laughter. He was so amused he didn't even paddle us for it.

Those days are long gone now, but certainly not forgotten. Often I picture Frog Lee sitting atop his desk and doling our words of wisdom. And I can't help but think of him every time I hear someone say, "It's not fair."

Plum Peculiar Perception

I just watched a movie titled Tucker and Dale vs. Evil. I kept seeing it listed on Netflix and finally my brother convinced me to watch it. It's a great movie. It's also a tad realistic in how city dwellers, especially those from anywhere besides the South, see rural southern folks.

In the movie, a group of college kids decide to camp out and come across two country fellows (Tucker and Dale) and immediately perceive them to be dangerous hillbillies, which of course couldn't be further from the truth. But that's the premise of the plot, and not far from reality.

I can give you an actual personal example of what I mean. Over a decade ago, when Maggie and I were doing the long distance dating thing, she planned to visit me in Alabama. That caused a lot of concern amongst some of her family members, especially her older sister Maria (My goddaughter's grandmother). Being the protective older sister, Maria called me before Maggie's trip to express her worries.

"Let me get this straight," I said. "You grew up in Chicago and live out near Los Angeles, two places with super high crime rates, and you're worried about Maggie coming to rural Alabama?"

It doesn't make sense when you think of it that way. Violent crime on Sand Mountain, at least in our neck of the woods, is almost nonexistent. Yet people from New York City, where murder, robbery, assault, and every other kind of violent crime happen on a regular basis and has become a part of their lives, think rural Alabama is the scarier place.

Movies probably have a lot to do with it. Let's face it, Deliverance even scared us southerners. You're never able to see Ned Beatty the same and who can forget the mountain man's infamous words: "He got a real pretty mouth ain't he?"

So let me address these concerns. If you're from out west or up north and find yourself traveling through rural Alabama and your car breaks down and you've lost your cell phone signal — beware. Someone is probably going to pull up behind you in an old pickup truck, call their cousin Cooter to come tow your car, take you to their house and feed you a home-cooked meal, and give you a sack of sandwiches after Cooter fixes your car. Oh, the horror.

Seriously, people think all we do in the South is sit around eating grits, eating watermelons, eating fried chicken, drinking sweet tea, going to church, going muddin', dating our relatives, and looking for UFOs.

Well let me set you straight. I do not drink sweet tea and second cousins don't count.

It's the Heat AND the Humidity

I had one task to complete Sunday. My yard is divided by a

long steep driveway and in the middle of the left section is a large ugly bush about seven feet high surrounded by rotting landscape timber. It even had a Polk Salad bush growing right up through the middle that topped off about ten feet high. (Granny would have loved that.) My goal was to rid my lawn of this eyesore.

A friend was coming over to help and I decided we should begin before it got too hot. We started at 8:00. By 8:05 I realized we should have started three hours earlier. In a matter of minutes, sweat was pouring off me in buckets. My shirt was soaked, my glasses stayed fogged over, and my eyes were burning.

Milwaukee has hot summers now. The older people up there talk about how much worse it has gotten, especially over the last decade. The thermometer tops the 100 mark frequently. But it's still a dry climate, so 100 degrees in Milwaukee is nothing compared to an 85 degree morning in Alabama. It's not even close.

I had forgotten what summers were like here. You've heard the expression: "It's not the heat; it's the humidity." Well in Alabama it's both. We are cursed with both heat and humidity, and they conspire with each other to make the weather unbearable.

We were able to finish the job. We cut away the limbs, took a chain and used my truck to pull up the root systems, covered it over with soil, and sewed the area with that grass patch stuff. By then it was a little after ten o'clock and my shirt, pants, socks, and even my shoes were soaked in sweat. After a shower and four huge Gatorades, I was feeling back to normal.

I recently opened a hot dog concession stand at Collinsville Trade Day. I think we have the best hot dogs on the planet, and you can have whatever you want put on them. But Saturday was our fifth weekend to be open, and so far our number-one best-seller is ice-cold bottled water. Some people walking by look like they're about to have a heat stroke.

Thank goodness my concession building is air conditioned. For that matter, thank goodness my life is air conditioned. My car has very cold air. The downstairs unit of my house keeps my home comfortable, and the upstairs unit will make you think you woke up somewhere above the Arctic Circle.

I know we ask this question a lot, but how did we do it? How did we survive our childhood without air conditioning?

Mom and Pop Stores

Times they are a changing. We say it all the time and nowhere is it more evident than the decline of mom and pop stores in this country. Many small retail establishments, which used to be family enterprises with the husband and wife running the entire operation, are slowly being replaced with franchise conglomerates.

Even rural general stores are giving way to chain convenient stores. I still remember the old stores, the dusty wood floors, the wooden shelves full of groceries, Coke coolers with the bottle top opener on the side, and always at least two old-timers playing checkers. And they just didn't play for fun; these guys were strategic geniuses.

I still say a cold Coca-Cola tastes much better from one of those old glass bottles than they do in the plastic bottles today. Plus, I miss getting ten cents for every bottled returned. Of course for my dad, it was always a R.C. Cola and Moon Pie.

Where we lived in Blake, our mom and pop store was the little place as you head off Sylvania Gap Road just past Westley's Chapel. When I was younger, it was owned by Gene Timmons, who had married one of my dad's cousins. Yes, it's hard to marry anyone on Sand Mountain who isn't one of our cousins.

And I still remember when I was a teenager and the store was purchased by one of the coolest couples I have ever known: Junior and Kathy Winkles. Kathy had been our bus driver, good old #207, and she was the best bus driver we ever had. No matter how many times she dragged me to the principal's office, I will always have fond memories of that lady.

Junior was the polar opposite of Kathy – loud and outspoken. I had the privilege of working with Junior when he drove a Coca-Cola truck. I was 13 and it was the first job I had outside of potato sheds. I loved every minute of it. It was hard work, but Junior made it so fun, it was hard to think of it as work.

"I'm running over to Winkles" was one of the most common phrases uttered around my house for many years. Of course "running" meant "driving." Rarely did we drive to the valley or back home without stopping at Winkles to get gas, snacks, milk, eggs, or tobacco.

I know it became Chambers after that and my cousin Angie Wells Buttram worked there for a while. I don't even know if it's still open. Things have changed so much since I lived there, but in my memory, I will always see a smiling Gene, Kathy with her hair up, or a laughing Junior behind the register of that old store.

E I E I O No

David Perea is an old friend from Fort Payne who I hung out with in our much younger and much wilder days. You may remember when his family owned Perea's Carpet in town. David still installs carpet, hardwood, tiles, and other types of flooring, but he has another interest these days too. He, his wife, and sons own Red Boat Farm.

It is the quintessential small old-fashioned heritage farm with tractors, gardens, barns, and all the animals a farm should have: turkeys, pigs, cattle, Guineas, chickens, goats, ducks, and donkeys. They often post pictures and videos of their animals, who they have named, especially when they have some new babies. All of his friends love it.

Many times I have watched his videos and found myself smiling at the relationship they have with their animals. Soon I find myself thinking how wonderful it must be to live on a farm. That's when my brain swings an imaginary hand, which smacks me on the back of my head, and I think, "Oh wait, I did live on a farm."

We had 30 acres and about 20 of that was a hog pasture. At

our peak we had about 100 hogs, but we only named the meanest and scariest ones, mostly for our protection. It was just easier to yell, "Here comes Meanie" than to yell, "Here comes that big sow who will try to bite your rear end off." The rest I simply referred to by a variety of four-letter words.

I detested everything about raising pigs from castrating new males to ringing noses. I also came to realize that not only were they the most stubborn animal on the planet, they were quite possibly the smartest. As Cliff Clavin explained on Cheers, if pigs had thumbs you could train them to do manual labor, and after 30 years on the workforce, at their retirement dinner you could eat them.

But the battles that would scar me for life, both physically and psychologically, were not the ones with the swine, but rather the ones with the barbed-wire and electric fences. I got shocked so many times by that fence that to this day I cannot stand even the mildest of electrical currents. I once tried those muscle stimulation devices and screamed like I was sitting in the electric chair.

In fact, I had a date recently and the lady informed me that if I was to get out of line, she was packing both a gun and a Taser. I looked her in the eye and said, "I would never not be a gentleman, but in case that was to happen, please use the gun."

Suppertime

My wife and I rarely eat together at home. On the weekends, I still love to make cheese omelets with bacon or sausage, grits, and biscuits. But Maggie likes to sleep late so I eat alone. When we both get off work during the week, I fix what I want and she does the same and we rarely eat at the table.

It was a lot different growing up in a large family on Sand Mountain in the 60s and 70s. Suppertime was when Mom called "Supper!" and we all sat at the table to eat. There was no going to eat in the living room to watch TV or get on the computer. It was just one of those things we did on a regular basis as a family.

When you grow up with something, you think of it as normal and assume everyone does everything the same. The first time in my adult life when friends invited me to dinner for spaghetti, I was surprised to see the noodles and dark brown sauce in separate servers. Mom's spaghetti was all mixed together when we got to the table, and it was orange. Seriously, it was orange. But man, was it good.

When we ate hotdogs, we used loaf bread. Buns were too expensive. To this day I don't buy hotdog buns. It's not that I can't afford them; they just don't taste right after eating plain bread with wieners for so long.

And when we had chili dogs, we would lay a slice of bread on a plate, add the wiener, mustard, ketchup, onions, then smother it with regular chili and eat with a fork. The first time I saw a chili dog in a bun with actual hotdog chili on it, I thought someone was playing a joke.

Pintos and cornbread was the most common meal we had. And although it wasn't my favorite dish by far, it must have become embedded in my DNA because now it is my favorite thing to have for supper. It might be because we rarely have it, but a plate of pintos with crumbled-up cornbread with raw onions and a glass of buttermilk is like heaven in my mouth.

Of course there were some things my mom made that I have never seen anywhere else. Salmon patties, for example, were kind of odd tasting, but we were thankful for whatever we had. But never in my life have I had a friend call up and say, "Hey, we're having salmon patties tonight. Wanna come eat?"

I hope most families with children still have suppertime and all eat at the table. It's not the food as much as the unity. Quality family time.

Once a Redneck

A year ago, a casting agent from Los Angeles contacted me and she was looking for potential stars for a new reality TV show titled "Redneck Intervention," later renamed "Redneck Rehab." Someone in New York had sent her my way, saying if she needed rednecks, I was the go-to guy.

She explained the premise of the show and sent me the video of the pilot. I came up with some possible candidates and they even went as far as to interview some people in Henagar and had them sign the waivers. But, alas, the show was cancelled after seven episodes.

Basically they were looking for people who had moved away from their redneck roots. She thought I would be a candidate, but after seeing the pilot, I knew I was not what they were looking for. They wanted people who had turned their backs on that whole lifestyle including their own kinfolk. The person in the pilot was actually embarrassed by her family.

That's when I knew I wasn't a fit. I'm still as much a redneck now as ever I was. I might not reside currently on the mountain, but the mountain resides in me. I've noticed that the farther away I am, and the longer I am away, the more the mountain calls to me and the more I miss my kin.

Sure, I have some cousins that might be considered a wee bit country. For example, my cousin J.W., I'm convinced his DNA is not entirely human, but part bloodhound. He's the only person I know who can find more rabbits than the dogs.

Once while we were hunting and the dogs were way ahead of us, he stopped walking and handed me his shotgun. I was confused but held it for him. He reached down in the leaves between his legs and pulled out a rabbit with his bare hands. The dogs had missed it, but not him. This is a true story.

I might not ever go rabbit hunting again, or frog gigging for that matter, or trot lining on the Tennessee River. I might not ever make another squirrel trap, corncob pipe, or cigarette made with Rabbit Tobacco. I might not ever swim again in the creek or catch crawfish. I might not ever again make home brew or muscadine wine. I might not ever again cut pulpwood or pick okra, and I really, really hope not as far as those two go.

But that's still home. That's the only place where everything makes sense. So even if the only thing I get to do when I make it home is spend a lazy afternoon sitting on the porch and chewing the fat with some of my kinfolk, it makes it all worthwhile.

All the Trimmings

My mom calls frequently to invite me to dinner: spaghetti, burgers, barbeque, etc. And although I'm usually tired and don't feel like driving all the way from south Fort Payne to Mom's house on Sand Mountain, I rarely turn her down. I wasn't sure why, but for some reason, Mom's food tastes so much better than mine.

My youngest sister lives in Henagar, an even farther drive, but it's the same when she invites me out. I couldn't put my finger on it before, but her meals also are so much better than the ones I prepare at my house.

My oldest sister lives less than a mile away, so I never refuse an invitation to have lunch or dinner there. The last time I was asked to eat there, I filled up on wonderful barbeque pork, a loaded baked potato, incredible coleslaw, and toasted garlic French bread. Yummy.

And it was at that very moment that it dawned on me why my mom's and sister's meals are so much better than the ones I prepare. It's all in the side items. It's all in the trimmings that complement the main dish.

Even when Mom makes burgers, she makes cheese burgers and has cut-up lettuce, sliced tomatoes, and sliced onions to decorate them. She will also have potato salad and coleslaw, or possibly macaroni and cheese, to round out the feast.

Having been on my own now for one year and four months, I have reverted back to my single guy days of eating. If I have chili or veggie soup one night for dinner, that's all I have. No side items, not even a peanut butter sandwich like you're supposed to have with chili or vegetable soup. We learned that in high school.

Sometimes I buy a microwavable tray of Salisbury Steak and that will be my dinner. I do use sliced bread to pour it over, but that is my only addition. No mashed potatoes, rice, or mac & cheese or anything.

Maybe that's why I still love breakfast most. I do breakfast right. My breakfasts, especially on the weekends, are a meal fit for a king, usually consisting of cheese omelets, real biscuits, sausage, bacon, gravy, and grits. As a Southerner, you can't just have eggs for breakfast. That's crazy.

But once breakfast is gone, I become the epitome of a single man living out of cans and boxes. I haven't turned on more than one stove eye for dinner since Christmas. And like a good hillbilly, sliced loaf bread serves many functions: hamburger buns, hotdog buns, hoagie buns, Texas toast, French toast, and everything else. That's the only trimming I ever get at home.

O Bama, Where Art Thou?

There are many things that elude the misplaced Southerner living up north, and it's not just manners and hospitality. There are also the food challenges. If you buy cornbread already made, for example, it tastes like cake. Crazy Yankees! If I wanted a cake, I would buy a cake.

I think most Southerners have traveled out of the South and seen that deer-in-the-headlights stare from servers in restaurants who say, "Sweet tea? There's sugar right there on the table if you want to put it in your tea." They just don't get it. Of course they don't make their tea with sugar; they used it all in their cornbread.

It took me a while but I finally found one store up here that sells grits and one store that sells Dale's Steak Sauce. The steak sauce was a delivery error and the people working there didn't even know what it was. No joke. But there's still one thing that cannot be found in any store in Milwaukee and it's a very important thing—Bama Mayonnaise. I can't eat a sandwich without it.

Every time I return from Alabama, my car is packed down with as many jars of Bama as I can fit around our luggage. It's a good thing I don't have kids or they might end up strapped down on top of the car as to leave more room for the mayo. It makes me feel like a bootlegger as I wonder what the legal limit is to bring it across the Mason-Dixon Line.

And it's still not enough. Just yesterday I frantically searched for my hidden, emergency stash. Even though I found it, I know it will not last until August when I return to the promised-land. I know what's coming next: the withdrawal pangs, the shakes, the cold sweats in the middle of the night as my body goes through detox. I'm a bona fide Bama Mayo junkie.

Many times, in desperation, I have driven around town looking for shady characters on dark street corners in every bad part of town hoping to score. Just once I dream that they will open their trench coats and reveal those beautiful jars with the blue tops filled with the right stuff. They'll smile and say, "Pssst, buddy, need some Bama?" But no, all they sell are drugs and stolen Rolex watches.

Soon my wife will wake in the middle of the night to strange sounds of me going through all our cabinets and compartments in the fridge hoping to find at least one little squeeze pack. "I'm sorry, Honey," I'll say with bloodshot eyes. "I need a hit."

Play Ball

It is 81 degrees today in Milwaukee and it's about time. I wasn't sure if this winter was ever going to end. But as we move toward summer, my thoughts abound with memories of softball. I loved playing baseball as a kid but I was mesmerized by women's softball.

There have been many great rivalries on the professional level throughout history, but none compare to the one that existed for at least a quarter of a century right there on Sand Mountain between the Sylvania Women's head coach and the Rainsville Women's head coach: Carthell Carlyle and Jerry Willingham.

All three of my sisters, Julene, Neenah, and Denise, played under Coach Carlyle and I think all three of them played under Coach Willingham as well. Both coaches built successful and competitive programs. I remember Coach Willingham walking with the aid of a cane, but can't remember why. Coach Carlyle seemed like an easy-going country fellow who would look just as home on a tractor as he did in the dugout.

Beth and Emily, Coach Carlyle's daughters, were staples in his lineup for many years, and both were talented athletes.

On Rainsville's side, I still remember Diane, the lady who pitched for Coach Willingham probably for decades. And I definitely remember the shortstop, Brenda Gulledge. Brenda was phenomenal. She could throw and hit as well as any guy I've ever known.

When these two teams met at the field in Rainsville or the field in Sylvania, you could feel the electricity in the air. As a kid I loved watching these games. I would only leave my seat to get a soggy hotdog and soda from the concession stand. Other than that, my bottom was glued to the bleachers.

I don't know how many total years these guys coached or what their overall records were, but they selflessly dedicated their time to providing an outlet for countless women athletes of all ages where I'm sure they learned a lot more than just how to play the game. I'm certain they all walked away with a few lessons on life as well.

These two coaches had to love what they did. How could they not? There was no pot of gold in it for them. All of the time they devoted to their players over the years had to come from something more powerful than financial gain. It was simply a part of them, who they were.

From a fan-in-the-stands point of view, it meant a lot to me. It's been many years now so I assume these two great coaches have since passed away. So, thank you. You guys made a difference in the lives of so many and I can't think of a better way to live a life.

Clunkers and Junkers

I've written before about how things we grow up with follow us into adulthood, like certain foods for example. I might be able to afford better cuisine, but hot dogs, cheap pizza, and potted meat sandwiches still dominate my menu. Another area of my childhood that has become a part of me is my inability to spend too much on anything with a motor.

Growing up on a small farm with limited finances meant we got by on the bare minimum when it came to internal combustion mechanisms. I remember the farm truck we had when I was about 12 years old. It was a 1949 one-ton flatbed Dodge. The starter button was located on the floor beside the brake pedal, which is where the headlight dimmer switch would be found in later models.

The only thing harder to drive than that old truck was our old Farmall tractor. It had the crank in the front and all the attachments were manual. When you got to the end of a row, you had to reach back and pull a giant lever to raise the plow. And this was when most farmers were riding in air conditioned John Deere models with full hydraulic systems.

Our cars were so cheap that when they broke down, it was easier to sell them for junk and buy another one rather than repair them. Our garden tiller was from the Great Depression era, and our lawnmower was so rusted the motor barely clung to the frame. It smoked profusely, which was good in case you ever ran over a Yellow Jacket nest.

Although I'm not quite as bad as my dad when it comes to cars, I've still never purchased a new vehicle. It just seems like a waste of money to me. Before I moved to Milwaukee, I tried to always pay cash for vehicles, which ruled out driving one off the showroom floor.

And while I did buy my lawnmower new, that was 14 years ago and I'm still using the same one. My snow blower, however, is a relic from the Cold War. It's a huge beastly thing that even my neighbors can't operate. I gave $75 for it seven years ago and it's still going strong, although the drive chain has begun to slip off the sprockets.

This past fall as I was patching one of the inner tubes, my wife asked me why I didn't just buy a new snow blower. "They're only about $700," she said. "Why don't we just get a new one?"

What a silly question. The answer is obvious. Why would I spend $700 on a new one when I can get a clunker for seventy-five?

Superstitious Much

We like to think we're not very superstitious, but I think deep down all of are to some degree. It's ingrained in our brains starting with our first birthday when we're old enough to blow out the candles. After all, if we blow them all out in one breath, our wish will be granted.

How many of you have made a wish on the first star of the evening, or a falling star, picked a four-leaf clover, rubbed a rabbit's foot, hung a horseshoe, or tossed a coin into a fountain? How many won't pick up a coin if it's not head's up?

A few days ago at the Depot a friend was helping us trim the Christmas tree. He handed me his open pocket knife to hold. When I handed it back to him, the blade was still open. When asked why I didn't close it, without even thinking I blurted out, "Because I didn't open it." I was taught as a kid that was bad luck and have never questioned it.

Bad luck superstitions probably outnumber good luck. To this day I still won't step on a crack as I'm walking down a sidewalk because I don't won't to be responsible for breaking my mother's back. I refrain from walking under ladders, try never to spill salt, hope a black cat doesn't cross my path, and I'm very careful not to break a mirror. I never rock an empty rocking chair and I don't run with scissors. Okay, I don't run these days at all.

The superstition regarding Friday the 13th, or the number 13 in general, reaches far beyond individuals. Over 80% of high-rises have no 13th floor, nor to most hospitals and hotels. Most airports are sans a 13th gate and airplanes have no 13th aisle. Italy has omitted 13 from their national lottery and in Florence the house between 12 and 14 is addressed as 12 ½.

And let's not forget superstitious itches. If just about any part of your body itches or burns, it means something. If your right ear itches, someone is speaking well of you. The opposite if it's your left ear. Right eye itching means a birth in the family, left eye means a death. If your nose itches, it means you will soon be kissed by a fool. My ex-wife's nose must have itched something terrible. And a sudden chill means someone just walked across your grave.

It might not be scientific but why take chances? I'll just continue the way I was brought up, which mean I won't put my ball cap on the bedpost at night, and I'll always spit on a new bat for luck.

This Is No Bull

My maternal grandmother, Lela Jackson, whom we all called "Granny," was quite the character. Most of us who grew up on the mountain back in that time probably had at least one older relative who was as country as country can be. Granny was ours. She cussed like a sailor, swore by a hundred home remedies, and always told it like she saw it.

I could fill a book with stories about this woman, like the time I came home to visit and noticed her 1963 Impala had a new paint job. This was surprising since Granny, even had she not been on a meager government allowance, was very thrifty. It became clearer as I neared the car and noticed the drips on the grass and could see the brush strokes. Yes, she had painted it herself.

I always made sure to visit her when I came home, mainly because I sincerely enjoyed her company. On one such visit I asked if she was still having problems with the bull that lived in the large pasture across the dirt road. It had been jumping the fence and partaking of her garden offerings. Granny shook her head. "Not a problem anymore."

Needless to say that answer activated my curiosity, and quite frankly, scared the crap out of me. I asked her to explain, so she continued. "He got in my garden again so I took my shotgun and fired into the air." She rocked in her chair and smiled as she relived the moment. "It worked. He jumped his butt right back over that fence."

I knew Granny's shotgun well. She had it since before I was born. It was an old timey double-barrel 12-guage with rabbit ears, which are the two hammers you pull back to make it ready to shoot. The thought of her actually firing this thing, which probably weighed more than she did, wasn't a pretty picture, but I was glad she only scared the bull.

Later when I got to Mom's house, I learned that Granny's story was only mostly true. She failed to mention that the air she shot into was the air between her and the bull, striking the fella on the rear haunches. No wonder he jumped back over the fence so quickly. Sadly the owner had to have him put down.

We were all thankful that the farmer declined to press charges. I think he understood that Granny was just an old country woman who didn't realize she had even done anything wrong. Maybe he was just trying to be a good Christian neighbor practicing forgiveness. Or maybe it was because he knew she still had the shotgun.

Put Out to Pasture

There are cow pastures all around DeKalb County and I drive

by without giving them a thought in the world, and I certainly have no desire to venture into one. But when I was a kid, I couldn't stay out of them.

Way back through the woods behind our house, and across the big fallen log that stretched across the creek, was a huge pasture that I sought out often. It was the best area to find arrowheads and other Native American artifacts. I could spend all day combing through the grass and flipping over rocks in search of these treasures.

And directly across from Granny's house was a huge pasture that was one my favorite places to pass the time during hot summer days. Deep in the middle were several huge ponds where few humans ever passed. They were full of fish and huge bullfrogs. I made many a midnight gigging trips, making sure to watch out for the hundreds of Water Moccasins that also lived there.

My favorite fishing hole was Buddy's Pond, owned by my kinfolk Buddy Wells, and you guessed it, it was in a pasture. I took Granny there many times and she loved it. I think we were the only ones he let fish there. We would catch our share of catfish and snapping turtles. I don't remember there being cows, but he had a goat that loved to climb on top of our car.

I never got into cow-tipping, but two of my cousins and I did invent our own nighttime pasture game. In the darkness we would walk slowly along with a large dip net. Suddenly we would stumble into a nest of sleeping field larks. They would fly up all around us and even into us, as we swung the nets wildly trying to catch them. I can't remember how many points we got for catching one, but that's moot since we never did.

And of course who could forget all the neighborhood softball games which always took place in the pasture. We had nowhere else that had that much flat surface for a field. We'd use someone's shirt or an extra glove to mark the bases then two captains would pick their teams. It was fun and quite adventurous. Rarely did we have a game where someone didn't slip on a cow pie.

Although being "put out to pasture" is a phrase that sums me up these days, in reality I doubt you'll ever catch me in a pasture again. But the lessons remain: Never enter a pasture with an ornery bull, watch out for prickly pears, and for goodness sakes don't pee on the electric fence.

Runs in the Genes

When I played football in high school, I was the fastest lineman on the team. I could run the 40-yard dash in 4.7 seconds. That's not Bo Jackson speed of course, but not bad for a stocky Sand Mountain pig-farmer whose legs were proportionately way too short for his body.

My first job out of high school was at the Shell Carwash in Fort Payne. There I would challenge many coworkers, many much taller coworkers, to a footrace, and watch their look of astonishment as someone of my limited vertical prowess outran them.

As fast as I was, however, my dad, Travis Wooten, was faster. At that time Dad was near 50 years old, smoked like a chimney, weighed about 250 pounds, and could smoke me. He used to love to challenge guys my age to a race, and when they yelled "Go," Dad would turn around and run backward and still outrun them.

It has to be a hereditary thing, because it goes back further than me and my dad. My grandfather, Pete Wooten, had it too. In fact, to hear Dad tell it, Pete was much faster than he was. That's hard for me to fathom, but others have verified this.

One day I was working at the carwash and an older gentleman came in to get gas. When he saw my name on my shirt, he asked if I knew Pete Wooten. When I explained that he was my grandfather, the man's eyes lit up and he began telling me stories.

"Pete was the fastest person I ever met. One time I watched him race a horse. A man rode the horse and Pete ran on foot. The horse won, but barely. We used to call him Greased Lightning because he was so fast."

I love hearing old stories about anyone, but especially about family. The old fellow told me several tales that day, including one

Dad had told me before. "Pete could stand behind a full-grown man and, without getting a run and go, squat down and leap completely over him."

The other thing the three of us had in common was that we all had humongous calf muscles and flat feet. And when I say "flat feet," I mean zero arch. When we walked barefoot on a dirt road, you could see our entire footprint.

I read once that people with flat feet can never be as fast as people with a good arch. Wow. If we had been born with arches, we might have been in the Olympics. I never knew Pete's dad, Van Wooten, nor have I heard stories about him, but I assume he was the Flash.

Tonie the Tigress

I've mentioned several teachers, coaches, and even bus drivers in several articles, and I truly believe that those of us who went to Sylvania, and probably those who attended all the small schools in DeKalb County, were lucky to have these people as part of our educational experience.

But there's one teacher that will always occupy the brightest spots of my memory — Mrs. Tonie Niblett. Although every teacher I had treated me with kindness, Mrs. Niblett was the first one to see more in me than a poor farm boy with a smart aleck personality.

My senior year she selected me to be her teacher's aide for Algebra. I was honored, and more than a little shocked. When I think of a teacher's aide, I think of those students who embody the rigorous discipline of academics, not a kid who spent more time in the principal's office than he did in class. But I loved it.

She convinced me to try out for the math team, so I did, and my scores were high enough to secure one of the few spots on the team. One of my greatest achievements in life came at the math tournament at Austin High School in Decatur when my individual score landed me in first place. My score was so high that my team also took home a first place trophy.

I never had plans after high school. I hadn't intended on going to college at all. I didn't think I was allowed. I assumed that was just for wealthy kids. But Mrs. Niblett explained how she also struggled financially and worked her way through school. Suddenly it seemed possible.

Who knows how my life would have turned out differently without this incredible teacher. Even the things I've accomplished in life that are not math related, like a comedy career and writing several award winning and best-selling books, are because I learned that anything is possible for anyone who wants it.

That's not to say that having Mrs. Niblett was all peaches and cream. Far from it. She was clearly the toughest teacher I ever had as well. We had to maintain and submit a notebook full of work every week, which counted as part of our grade. I hated that. And math team practices I would rank somewhere between waterboarding and having your toenails ripped out.

I still have nightmares thinking I don't have my notebook ready to turn in. I think I need a psychiatrist, or perhaps a priest, someone who can help me exorcise the redheaded demon that haunts my soul.

But it was worth it. I'm sure I'm not the only one whose life was blessed for having her as a teacher.

Armed and Dangerous

Yay. The fair is coming to town. I have a special reason to be excited this year. Last year I went with my mom and it was great. That marked the first time I had been to the VFW Fair since before I moved away.

I still remember that time. I had just turned 18 and was going to Northeast. After I finished my last class and was walking toward the parking lot, I noticed they were having a blood drive. I figured it was a good cause so I donated a pint. "Don't do anything strenuous for the rest of the day," they said as I left.

It was the first time I had given blood and it wore me out. When I got home, I fell asleep on the sofa. Mom woke me when she got home from work and said, "Don't forget, you have the arm wrestling competition at the fair tonight."

Oh crap. I had forgotten. I can remember things that happened 40 years ago with no problem, but I can never remember things I'm supposed to do today. But I loved arm wrestling and was excited when they announced there was going to be a competition at the fair that year. Short a little blood and a lot of common sense, I still went.

This was 1983 and past the heyday of the arm wrestling craze from the late 70s, but the event still drew a lot of competitors from all over. Among them was the Georgia State Champion, a stocky, bearded guy who was shorter than me and wore elevated shoes to give him an advantage. He was kind of scary.

When they called my name for my first match, I took off my sweatshirt and wore my t-shirt. I beat the first man easily. As I walked away from the table, the announcer said something that still sticks in my memory. "Well, folks, it looks like Neal Wooten came to arm wrestle and he brought a set of arms with him." I blushed.

The competition progressed with neither the Georgia State champ nor I losing a match. The final came down to us. He was a tad intimidating as we locked hands. When they signaled us to begin, it was an immediate stalemate. The veins in his forehead were protruding making him look scarier.

I glanced down at the Band-Aid I still wore from giving blood and was afraid it would go flying off as a stream of blood shot into the guy's eyes. That would probably be grounds for disqualification. But alas, it didn't and I was able to prevail and win first place in the competition. I blushed.

Hillbilly Cuisine

My wife and I sure have our differences. For example, Maggie loves the opera and ballet. I'm more of a rodeo and monster truck show kind of guy.

Another place we differ is when it comes to places to dine out. I'm happy with a $6 Chinese buffet, whereas Maggie likes those fancy restaurants. And by fancy, I mean the ones with fancy lighting, fancy tables, fancy waiters, and of course fancy prices.

At one such establishment, I noticed a rather odd item on the menu—Cow Tongue. When Maggie suggested I try that, I said, "I don't think I want to taste something that's going to taste me going down." Not to mention how sad it made me feel thinking of all those cows in the pasture that could no longer "Moo" properly.

But it got me to thinking about what makes a food classified as classy, and what makes a food considered to be hillbilly? There sure seems to be a lot of similarities.

Like one time I noticed turtle on a menu also. Heck, growing up on Sand Mountain, I must have snagged dozens of big old snapping turtles while fishing for catfish with liver. I'd drop them off at Aunt Edna's and she'd skin 'em and fry 'em right up. My favorite section was the neck. And yes, it did taste like chicken.

I've read that frog legs are also a delicacy at your finer diners. That's another thing I had plenty of growing up. When I was about 14, one of my cousins and I went frog gigging every Saturday one summer and brought back a bag full of bullfrogs each time. We'd munch away on fried frog legs while watching "Shock Theater" every Saturday night.

So, when I was a kid, was I just an uppity hillbilly without knowing it? I can't remember ever sticking out my pinky when eating real fried pig skins or mountain oysters. It seems the difference in hillbilly food and classy food is in the way you acquire it. If you go to the woods or the water and get it yourself, well, that's just backwards. But if you pay a man in a penguin suit a small fortune to bring it to you, that's real class.

That seems a little hypocritical to me. I know this, if I ever see "Fried Potted Meat" on a menu, I'll know I'm home. I'll stick out my pinky finger and ask for some Grey Poupon.

Just Desserts

I definitely have a sweet tooth, as did my dad, and as do a lot of my family. Growing up, however, we seldom had desserts after meals. The only time we had it on a semi-regular basis was for breakfast when we would have a can of sorghum syrup, bought from a guy at Taco-Bet, to mix with butter and sop up with a biscuit.

Mom always made sure to have a cake for her kid's birthday parties, so that was at least five times a year we had that. And of course the holidays called for sweets. Easter and Halloween came with candy; homemade ice cream for the Fourth, and Thanksgiving and Christmas wasn't complete without homemade banana pudding.

Thinking back, I realize most of the sweets we had way back then were hardly ever store-bought. We would walk for miles gathering wild blackberries just so Mom would make blackberry jam. Or we would gather plums or muscadines so Mom could make jelly.

And both Mom and Dad could make peanut brittle as good as any you can find in stores. Mom also occasionally would make candy peanuts, which was pretty simple. Just add raw peanuts and sugar to boiling water. As the water evaporates, the sugar, which turns pink from the peanut skins, adheres to the nuts making candy-coated peanuts.

Nature provided us with a lot of sweet snacks as well. Many times the blackberries, muscadines, and plums didn't make it all the way home. I can still feel the juice running down my chin from biting into a plump ripe plum. Along with Mom's strawberry patch and Dad's watermelon garden, there were natural desserts all over the place.

Sucking the nectar from honeysuckles was another great way

to get a quick sweet fix in the summer, or chewing on the twig of a sweet gum tree.

Of course, who needs that anymore? Now all you need to do is go to the store and pick out your favorite sweet from the thousands available. Forget all that homemade and natural stuff. Get you some Ferrous Sulfate, Thiamine Mononitrate, Riboflavin, Folic Acid, Dextrose, Partially Hydrogenated Vegetable Oil, Soy Lecithin, Phosphates, Mono and Diglycerides, Polysorbate 60, Sodium Stearoyl Lactyiate, Calcium Caseinata, and Yellow Die #5.

Yum! How did we live without all these great-sounding things for so long? And for the record, I took these items from the list of ingredients in a Twinkie.

People my age love to talk about how much fitter we were than kids today and how we stayed outside and played all day. But I wonder, can we really take credit for that? I don't remember my parents or grandparents ever filling me full of stuff like this.

Mountain Cold

Sure, I just moved back to the South after living for a decade in Wisconsin. Yes, it snowed a lot up there and the temperatures could plummet. But as the year winds down in Alabama, I'm reminded that Old Man Winter doesn't exactly take the season off here either. It was 16 degrees as I traveled to Trade Day Saturday morning.

I remember my childhood and sleeping under about ten blankets and quilts on winter nights. The alarm would go off to signal time to get ready for school, and besides turning the alarm off, I couldn't move. The living room was the only room with heat, so I had to muster the courage to jump out from under the covers and make a mad dash to the wood-burning heater.

Waiting on the school bus was also painful as your breath exhaled in thick plums of mist, which made it look like you were smoking. The windows on the bus would be frosted over. We used to make designs by pressing our hands up against the glass to melt away the ice. And those green vinyl seats were unforgiving.

My wife learned the hard way about the cold of the mountain. One winter while we were visiting, it was a very cold and wet day. Maggie, who grew up in Chicago, couldn't understand it. "I have on three coats and I'm still freezing," she complained. We had to explain about the humidity.

Mom called me several nights ago to say something I haven't heard or even thought about in a very long time. "I had to keep my water running last night," she said. I had forgotten how often we had to do that on the mountain to keep our pipes from freezing.

In Milwaukee, it's almost unheard of for pipes to freeze. I think it has to do with the dry climate. You can leave a two-liter coke outside on the coldest days up there and the liquid will not freeze. Open the lid and it suddenly freezes solid. On the mountain that bottle would be a solid chunk of ice without having to open it.

And our car windshield never iced over during the night up there. It's almost every morning here that I have to scrape away the frost to be able to see where I'm driving. I now recall that I used to place a piece of cardboard under my windshield wiper on the driver's side. Anyone else do that?

So I'm glad to be back and very glad I won't be shoveling any snow – ever again. But if it's just the cold that you hate, don't move to Sand Mountain. Just stay in Wisconsin.

The Days That Are No More

As I get older, I realize that many of the fun events that are scattered throughout my memory will remain just that – a memory. It's not just that I've grown too old or that I've moved far away; some things are simply gone forever.

Sequoyah Caverns was one of my favorite places to take friends from other areas. I loved the deer and bison, the gift shop with Indian artifacts, and the tour of the cavern itself. I remember one year they held the haunted house inside the caverns and that was awesome. I will certainly miss that place.

I can't count how many times I went to the old Hamilton drive-in theater in Fort Payne, from going as a kid with my family, to riding my motorcycle there with cousins and friends. Driving around that little dirt road and seeing that huge structure that was the screen was as much fun as seeing the movies.

Stopping by Jacks to get a Bonanza Burger was as common as breathing the air. Owned by Jack Locklear back in the day, one of my dad's favorite cousins, nothing beat a burger, fries, and a vanilla milkshake from Jacks. Whenever I come back to visit now, I have to run by The Strand just to get a replica Bonanza Burger for nostalgia sake.

One of our favorite places to swim is Desoto Falls. Every summer I would take my brother and sisters up there many times to cool off in the deep waters by the dam. Afterwards, on the way home, we always stopped at this little dairy farm for handmade ice cream. It was delicious. Many years ago, after a visit to the falls, I noticed the dairy was closed. Does anyone else remember that place?

Now Kmart in Fort Payne has closed or is closing. I don't remember the date. I worked at that store for three years before moving to Montgomery. There were a lot of great people there and I tried to get by and visit them when I would come home. Most of them remember the crazy Kmart robbery and love to laugh about it.

I know things can't last forever, but whenever we lose a place from earlier in our lives, it just reinforces the knowledge of our own mortality. It reminds us that we're all getting older and nothing can stop that.

Sometimes I wish I could turn back the clock if only for a day. If I could have one day, I would visit all the places from my memory and end the day eating Bonanza Burgers and handmade ice cream watching episodes of Shock Theater.

All Our Yesterdays

Here's a crazy memory that sticks in my mind. I was 12, which means my dad would have been 42, and we were at a farmer's market selling a truckload of Silver Queen corn. Dad was talking with two older farmers who appeared to be in their 70s.

The conversation they were having, one a lot of people have, and one I've written about here from time-to-time, was about the proverbial good old days. "When I was a young man," one of the fellows said, "I could work one day and make enough money to buy a brand new pair of overalls."

"And how long did you have to work back then?" my dad asked, never being one to simply agree with someone else. "Sunup to sundown," the farmer proudly exclaimed. "Well today," Dad replied, "most people only have to work eight hours a day and make enough to buy two pair of overalls."

The old men looked at my dad like he was crazy. They stood for several seconds with blank expressions until walking off to find someone who could better understand their logic.

I am guilty of this. I use the phrase "back in my day" often, and always to show how much better things were. Why do we do this? It is simple prejudice -- mine is better than yours, or do our brains instinctively hold on to only the good memories, making us believe those days were better than they actually were?

I hear friends say, "When I was a kid, I played outside all day long." Of course we did because it was much hotter in the house. We knock children today for their hobbies, but trust me, if I had grown up with central air, internet, big screen TV, and awesome video games, I'm sure my answer would have been different when my cousins called wanting to play Hide-and-Seek.

Most folks my age miss their first car, that 1970-something gas-guzzler, but don't realize how much they really prefer the newer, more economical, more technological, safer models of today. We complain about not finding anything good to watch with our 200-channel programming as if 40 years ago our three channels somehow provided the perfect shows all day long.

Sure society has changed and children today don't act like they did when I was a kid, but that's inevitable. Every generation since this country was founded has witnessed that. But if I'm honest, I can admit that life today is much easier than it was when I was a kid. So have heart. As Billy Joel said, "The good old day weren't always good, and tomorrow ain't as bad as it seems."

A Skipping Memory

The more time passes, the clearer my memory becomes. I remember events from high school in perfect detail. Just don't ask me what I had for breakfast this morning. One memory that remains crystal clear is a day from my senior year at Sylvania when three friends and I decided to skip class. We hid out at the field house. Glenn Graham was there, but he was the only one supposed to be there.

About halfway through the period we looked out the front door and saw the principal, Weldon Parrish, headed right down the middle of the gridiron. I swear that man was part blood hound. The four of us who were skipping class ran into the equipment room. I hid behind the open door and could see into the main room through the gap, and Buster Waldrop dove into the huge box made of plywood where odd football pads were kept.

I watched as Mr. Parrish walked up to Glenn and greeted him. "Glenn, I'm looking for four boys who are skipping class." Then he called us by name. "Have you seen them?" Glenn shook his head. "No sir, I haven't." And right there that boy went up several notches in my book.

Mr. Parrish didn't pressure him. In fact, he didn't mention us again, only stood there by Glenn talking about the weather, the football season, the Middle East, and who knows what else. It was making me very nervous. Why did he keep hanging around? At that moment I got my answer.

Buster, who couldn't see or hear anything from inside that wooden box, and was most likely running out of fresh air, pushed the lid up about six inches and yelled, "Is he gone?"

A smile crept across Mr. Parrish's face as he looked into the equipment room. Surely we were all doomed. But now it wasn't just us in trouble, but the one who had lied for us. Weldon Parrish looked back at Glenn, still with the huge smile, and said, "I'll ask you one more time, Glenn. Have you seen these boys?"

Glenn was busted. There was nothing left to do but rat us out and save his own skin. And we wouldn't have even held it against him. But Glenn never wavered. He stood as straight as an oak tree, looked our principal in the eye and said, "No sir, I haven't seen them."

Mr. Parrish's smile got bigger. He stared at Glenn for several seconds then patted him on the shoulder. "Okay then." At that he walked out the door and back up the football field. To this day I'm not sure why. I think he was just so impressed with Glenn, but not as much as I.

Been There, Done That

Technology has certainly passed me by. Young folks today definitely have the upper hand when it comes to using today's gizmos and gadgets. It's true that I'm from the proverbial old school. But when the apocalypse finally happens, be it from nuclear war or a zombie outbreak, I'll be the one who survives.

I've learned to do things that the younger generation has not. For example, I know how to siphon gas and drive a stick-shift. When all the car batteries are dead, I'll know how to push a vehicle down a hill to get it started. So while all the millennials are walking, I'll be cruising in a 1975 flatbed truck. I'll even know the dimmer switch is beside the clutch.

I've used a water bucket to get drinking water. Just lower that long, slim metal tube down into the well until you hear it fill up then crank that rope and bring it back up. Then hold it over a bucket and pull the metal ring on top to release. We have one in the museum and I'm surprised how many people who are much older than I am ask me what it is.

I know how to build, and use, an outhouse. I've heard folks say they used one when they visited their grandparents, but I grew up using one every day. So while the younger folks are out there wiping with a batch of poison oak, I'll be sitting in luxury. The one we had was a two-seater. You can't hide money.

While the whippersnappers are scrounging for scraps and bugs to eat, I'm going to have a big beautiful garden. I never thought I would enjoy growing my own food after my youth, but living for a decade in Milwaukee proved me wrong and that my green thumb was alive and well. The hardest part of the apocalypse will be not being able to post my tomatoes on Facebook.

I know how to fiddle worms. I can make a fishing rod, spear, and frog gig out of small trees. I know how to catch crawfish using tin cans. I can make a trot line and know how to use empty jugs to catch fish and I can build a fire without matches. I might just have an all-you-can-eat catfish buffet every night.

I grew up using all manual tools from drills to handsaws. Heck even today, I've never used a nail gun in my life. All of those things I thought were so hard to learn to do as a kid, might just have been preparing me for the future. So bring on the apocalypse. I have my kerosene lamp ready.

Country Bumpkins

Most of our cousins grew up right there on Sand Mountain and were just as simple and country as we were. But we had some that were from Fort Payne and some from larger towns like Chattanooga. And we had some from large cities in Georgia and North Carolina.

These cousins were always a little… different.

We didn't see them as much, but when we did, it was always an experience. They seemed more sophisticated, worldly, and knowledgeable, especially about grownup things. They had been around. And they looked at us like we were the most backward silly hillbilly doofuses on the planet.

"What do you even do for fun around here?" I must have heard that a hundred times growing up, but it's a trick question. Don't answer it. Sure, you could explain to them about how many great fishing spots there are, or about frog gigging, camping out, playing hide-n-seek, and a lot of other great activities, but they only laugh.

And to be honest, I was sometimes a little embarrassed. When these cousins would talk about all the exciting things to do in the cities, I was a tad jealous. I wanted those things. Sometimes I wondered why anyone would intentionally live in a small rural town.

Of course this was back when I was a kid. Having now been around the block a few times myself, I now understand the appeal of life on the mountain. Now I would gladly trade the sound of traffic for the sound of a Hoot Owl, or the crowded neighborhoods for the wide open spaces.

Sure, I can literally walk to Miller Park and watch the Braves take on the Brewers. We have giant water parks and amusements parks a few minutes away. We have tons of restaurants and theaters and just about anything you can imagine. But I would trade any of those for a quiet cookout on a nice front porch with a several friends and relatives.

When I was a teenager, I dreamed of getting away and seeing the world, or at least a little more of it. Now my goal is to make it back to the mountain, perhaps build a small house on our property on Sand Mountain and just let the mountain air remove all of the city stress.

I still hope to get visits from my city relatives, but it will be different this time. When they laugh at me and call me a big old country bumpkin, I'll just smile right back and say, "You better dang well know it."

Can I Go?

When you grow up at the end of a dirt road on a small farm on Sand Mountain surrounded by woods and your days are spent tending to hogs or picking crops, getting away from the house was a rare but welcomed event. That's why no matter where my mom was going when I was a kid, I wanted to go too.

Even the laundromat, which looking back on now was perhaps the most boring thing ever, was a delightful change of pace. Mom's favorite laundromat was in that brick building near the South Y in Fort Payne near DeKalb Auto Parts. If I had a dime on me, I'd go next door and buy a comic book at the convenience store. That would keep me happy until time to load the clothes and go home.

I would even go shopping with Mom when she went to buy clothes, something I will not do now with any woman. I have fond memories of Bargain Town USA, which was on 3rd Street and Gault Ave in Fort Payne next to Westmoreland Tires. Do you remember that? There's a Dollar General there now, but I loved the old Bargain Town store.

And if those bargains weren't good enough, Mom would stop by the "Junk" store, which was at the end of Airport Road across from where Kmart used to be. Thinking back, I assume it was actually a charity-based thrift store, but we called it the Junk Store. I just remember the old clothes being piled so high on the floor you had to wade through them. That place was magical to me.

Heck, just going to the grocery store beat hanging around home. I'd follow Mom around the store as she grabbed each item off the shelves, watch as she read the info on each label as if she didn't purchase the same items every week, and head to the checkout.

If it was driving to pay bills, shop, or even go to Dr. Gibson's office when she was sick, I wanted to tag along. Maybe I enjoyed it because it was voluntary. The things I had to do with my dad, like cutting firewood and pulpwood, going to the fields, setting up at the Chattanooga farmer's market, and a slew of other not-so-fun activities, were not an option at all.

And this could be the reason that I'm such a homebody today. Thanks to Mom, I've been everywhere and seen it all. Who needs to go to places like Cancun, Las Vegas, or the Bahamas when you've spent all that time at the laundromat and Bargain Town?

Fishing With Granny

As spring approaches, I remember one of my favorites past times as I was growing up and even well into my adult years: taking my grandmother fishing. Granny, as we called her, was my mom's mother and lived on the same little dirt road we did and when it got warmer weather, she was ready to fish.

Our favorite spot was Buddy's Pond, owned by a relative, Buddy Wells. It was in one of his pastures and we could catch yellow (mud) catfish all day long, and the occasional snapping turtle. We ate both.

I remember the time we took Granny to one of those catfish farms where you pay by the pound and where the ponds are so crowded with fish that you can catch one right after the other. She loved it. But these fish were a little bigger than the yellow cats, most weighing around five or six pounds, and Granny lacked the strength to reel them in. Not a problem. She simply took her pole and walked away from the water's edge until she dragged the fish up onto the bank.

I recall the last time I ever took Granny fishing. It was behind my mom and dad's house at my dad's small pond. Granny's favorite bait for catfish was chicken liver, and she would never cut it into smaller pieces. She's put the entire thing on her hook and give it a heave, figuring I guess if she couldn't catch a fish, perhaps she could knock one unconscious.

This summer day I had brought along a large cooler of drinks and snacks. As we sat next to each other on opposite ends of the cooler, she went to throw out her line. Her reflexes had begun to wane a little in her later years, so her timing was a little off and the hook, line, and sinker went straight up.

I was not wearing a shirt and that big slimy glob of chicken liver landed on my back right square between my shoulder blades, then proceeded to ooze downward until it fell over onto the top of the cooler. Granny finally saw it and smiled. "Look where that landed," she said.

"I know dang well where it landed," I replied, turning my back so she could see the slime trail. "Now wipe that off." Granny laughed so hard she almost fell off the cooler.

I can't go fishing to this day without thinking of Granny sitting on the bank in her flannel shirt, even on the hottest days, sweat pants, and big old fishing hat. Those were some of the best days of my life and I can't wait to fish with her again.

"Hey Y'all, Watch This"

Ah yes, the famous last words of a true redneck, and never there be one dumber than I. My knees have paid the price for my lack of common sense for the last 30 years.

It began at the football game between us (Sylvania) and Fyffe in 1983, when I got the ligaments and cartilage torn in my right knee. A few surgeries later, you would think I would have the smarts to take care of that knee, but you'd be wrong.

I hurt it again water skiing, in Karate, power lifting, jumping off a train trestle over Little River Canyon, in a motorcycle wreck, and once when an inebriated friend said, "I bet you won't jump off the top of this here barn."

I went snow skiing for the first time in the Smokey Mountains when I was 25. After a ten minute class, I was ready for the slopes. After several successful trips down the beginner slope, I headed for the expert slope. Why not after all? I had about an hour of experience.

Turns out, going down the steep slope was not that difficult.

What I found challenging was stopping, and I was quickly approaching a ton of skiers at the bottom including women and children. I decided to perform what they referred to in class as a "controlled fall."

Apparently that doesn't work at 50 miles-per-hour. My skis and poles went in four directions, as did my bad knee. As I laid there screaming in agony, an instructor rushed to my aid. "Is it a broken leg?" he asked.

"No," I replied, "it's torn ligaments and cartilage."

"Wow," he said. "Are you a doctor?"

Now, 30 years later, I have finally learned to take it easy. The problem is it doesn't take crazy stunts to injure my knee anymore; it takes simple things like walking up steps, or just walking some days.

During my last visit to the doctor, he handed me a piece of paper. When I asked him what it was, he said it was an approval slip to obtain a handicap parking placard. I was stunned. It's something I never imagined I would do. It stayed on my desk for months, but I finally mailed it in.

Now it's official. I have the blue rectangular thing that hangs on my mirror. When it arrived in the mail, I looked at my wife and said, "OK, this is just for emergencies, like when I have a really bad knee day, or maybe at Christmas and we can't find any other parking space."

She agreed. And from that day several months ago, to this very day, we have used it every single time we leave the house. I'm so pathetic. If only I had the maturity in my youth to not yell, "Hey y'all, watch this."

Twang

I hate watching TV shows or movies that are set in Alabama. The accents are exaggerated and usually sound like someone who is undereducated and simpleminded, regardless if the actor is portraying a mechanic or a doctor. The speech is often delivered in a slow deliberate drawl.

While watching a movie like this a few weeks ago, my wife asked me if I knew anyone in Alabama who spoke like that. I told her no and explained that this was hardly an accurate depiction of how we speak.

The best way I can describe the accent of Alabama, and especially Sand Mountain, is to say it has a twang. It rises up with a hint of joy, a sound full of personality that lets you know the person is genuinely talking to you and not at you. I know very few people who talk slowly. Heck, some talk so fast I have to make sure I'm paying close attention to catch every syllable.

It's not just our language; it's also the food. I can't tell you how many people have asked me to explain why Bama Mayonnaise is the only brand I eat. It's kind of hard to put into words. The best I can do is to tell them that Bama has a twang to it. It's not bland and it's not spicy, it just has the right twang.

It's the same reason us Southerners soak our steaks, pork chops, ribs, and venison in Dale Sauce. It gives it that twang.

My wife was under the impression that everyone in the south liked their foot hot and spicy, noting that people in New Orleans ate their food this way.

I had to clarify that New Orleans is not the South; it only rests in the southern part of the United States. Being Southern is not only about geography. If you don't believe me, drive down into Florida and the farther south you get, the farther from Dixie you'll realize you are.

Being Southern is a philosophy, an attitude full of pride, passion, family, and good old Southern hospitality. It's about helping your neighbors, cookouts, and skinny-dipping in the creek. It's about hot summers and cold sweet tea. It's about reunions, parades, and community involvement. It's about giving 'em hell on Saturdays pulling for your favorite college football team and thanking God for that and everything else on Sunday.

In short—it's all about the twang.

What's That Mean?

Growing up in the South when I did and hearing a lot of old timers speak normal conversation back in the day, means that naturally a lot of those old expressions have stuck with me ever since. Needless to say that oftentimes I have confused my nephews and nieces with phrases they don't understand, not to mention the Yankees in Milwaukee.

Many are easy to figure out, like "Hold your horses" or "Don't count your chickens before they hatch." Some I've had to explain like "Too big for your britches" and "Don't put the cart before the horse." But there were some I grew up hearing that even I wasn't clear on the origin. Here are some of those.

Madder Than a Wet Hen. I knew this referred to when a woman was very angry, but I had to investigate the actual beginning. Turns out farmers used to dunk hens in cold water to break their spirit so they could collect their eggs without the hens attacking them. So imagine how angry a hormonal hen is after an ice bath.

You Look Rode Hard and Put up Wet. No, this isn't dirty Southern innuendo. It refers to a key step in horse grooming. When a horse runs fast, it works up a sweat, especially under the saddle. A good rider knows to walk the horse around so it can dry off before going back to the stable. A horse will look sick and tired if you forget this step.

Drunk as Cooter Brown. Cooter Brown is an infamous character in Southern lore. Legend has it he lived on the Mason-Dixon Line during the Civil War. To avoid the draft on either side, Cooter decided to stay drunk throughout the entire war, making him ineligible for battle. Inebriated Southerners have measured their drunkenness by him ever since.

Finer Than Frog Hair. This phrase reportedly originated in C. Davis' Diary of 1865. We mostly use it to answer the question, "How are you?" People up north may not realize, but we Southerners know frogs don't have hair at all, so the irony means to highlight just how dandy we feel.

Happy as a Dead Pig in Sunshine. When a pig dies and lies outside a while, the sun dries out its skin. This effect pulls the pig's lips back to reveal a toothy "grin," making it look happy even though it's dead. So this phrase describes not only a person who is happy, but one who is blissfully ignorant of reality.

These are just a few. There are more than you can shake a stick at. And, the good Lord willing, I will continue to confuse the heck out of my nephews and nieces until the cows come home.

What's in a Name?

It is sometimes said that naming a location in the simplest direct terms is often the most effective. A fancy restaurant that caters to the who's who of Boston comes to mind. It was called The Café. Likewise, here in the South, we often follow that format.

The Hole in the Rock. This used to be one of my favorite places. As a kid I spray-painted my name there like so many other locals. The last time I drove by the old dirt road leading down to the cave, however, it was closed. Does anyone know if it still is? But it was basically a large hole in the side of the rock face of Sand Mountain, so it was aptly named.

Dead Man's Curve. I grew up hearing horror stories about this patch of road on Hwy 11 out past the airport. A few months ago I was driving through there in the pouring rain and immediately realized those stories might be true. The water was pooling up right in the curve and my big truck with oversized tires suddenly hydroplaned. It scared the crap out of me.

Joe's Truck Stop. For anyone reading my articles who are not from this area, let me explain. Years ago a fellow named Joe grew weary of 18-wheelers coming off Lookout Mountain on Hwy 35 and losing their brakes, something that was pretty common back then, and driving through his house. So he constructed a stone/concrete wall in front of his property about four feet high to stop them. It worked.

The Barn. Do you remember this nightclub in Scottsboro that opened way back when the town first went wet? I went there once and ran into a girl from high school. She asked me to sit at her table because someone kept throwing ice at her. I was obviously not a deterrent since it continued to happen with me there. Finally I changed seats with her and discovered the big air conditioning unit in the wall above the seat was dripping.

Even places that have longer, more descriptive names are usually shortened to a more common word or phrase that is used amongst locals. Before Scottsboro went wet, it was normal to hear someone say they were going to the line. They didn't have to say the DeKalb County/Etowah County line. We knew where it meant and why they were going.

We know "the river" is the Tennessee, "the lake" is Weiss, "the beach" is Gulf Shores, "the mountain" is Gatlinburg, "the canyon" is Little River, and "the bakery" used to be Merico, then Earthgrains, then Sara Lee. Now I have to send this to "the paper."

School's Out

We've had a lot of school-age kids come in the Depot Museum in the last few days, and I knew what that meant -- school is out for the summer. Of course I know more teachers now than I do students and they have all been counting down on Facebook with unbridled enthusiasm. When I was a kid I never realized that teachers looked forward to summer break as much as we did, maybe more.

When I was in school, the last day of school was more exciting than Christmas Day. I've never been in prison (not that I would tell you if I have) but I'm certain the feeling of taking that final bus ride home of the school year is comparable to being released from the slammer, the big house, the stir, and whatever other names it might be called since I have no idea about that.

I would stare out the bus window and feel totally free as my mind raced with thoughts of swimming, fishing, camping out, and sleeping late. I'd sing along with songs the other kids would be regaling with joy. "School's out, school's out, teachers let the monkeys out. No more pencils, no more books, no more teachers' dirty looks. School days, school days, finished with the golden rule days."

Oddly enough, I didn't know until just now when I Googled these lyrics, to make sure I had them right, that this is from an actual song titled "School's Out" by a fellow named Dan Bern. See, out of school for decades and I'm still learning.

Growing up beside first cousins who were a little older was a blessing. J.W., Roy, and Betty Sue could all drive before I could and they all knew where the best swimming holes and fishing spots were. And combined with me and my two older sisters, Julene and Neenah, we always had plenty of participants for Hide & Seek, Kick the Can and Run and Hide, Red Rover, Flies and Skinners, and a host of other fun games.

Summers always meant something else to me – money. I spent many summer days bailing hay, cleaning chicken houses, and working at potato sheds. But it was the summer when I turned 13 that I got my first "real" job, working on a Coca-Cola truck with Junior Winkles. I was walking in high cotton making $50 per week.

It's too bad we don't have this as adults. Wouldn't it be nice if we could all just take off work for the summer? Can you imagine the final drive home before summer break? "No more timeclocks, no more work, because my boss is a big fat jerk."

Off the Grid

I often read posts on Facebook of people saying they want to live off the grid. I'm not talking about like on those TV shows where some celebrity installs solar panels and wind turbines and continues to live the same comfortable life; I mean like in a small cabin in the woods with no electricity or running water.

It's a romantic notion I guess, to grow a garden for vegetables, hunt and fish for meat, chop wood for heat, and wash your clothes in the creek, but I don't think people know how horrible that would be after living with modern conveniences. Some of the people I see posting this are the same ones who go crazy when they lose their cell phone signal for five minutes.

As for me, I want my grid. I need my grid. I have no illusions about it at all because I've been there, done that. When I was growing up, we often would go long periods of time without electricity, not because we lived in a remote cabin, but apparently because the power company expected the bill to be paid every single month. I know -- crazy.

If you've never had to do your homework by the light of a kerosene lamp, you haven't lived a full life. (Sarcasm) You could see every place in our house where we positioned our lamps because it turned the wall and ceiling black. And I shudder to think of how many episodes of Hee-Haw we missed during those times.

Our electric heaters would lie dormant as we relied solely on an Ashley wood-burning heater. This thing put out a lot of heat, but we had only one in the living room. I remember waking on school mornings, covered with about eight blankets and quilts, trying to work up the courage to jump up and make a mad dash to the living room without getting frostbite.

Coming home from school meant carrying four empty milk jugs down into the hollow to fill with water from a spring. It sure was awesome drinking water. As soon as I moved away to college, I realized how much I missed that water. But again, if you've never had to heat water atop a wood-burning heater to be able to take a bath, you don't know what you're missing.

So to all those wanting to move to a shack and live off the grid, I say go for it. Chop you some wood, grow you a garden, get you some chickens for fresh eggs, and live happily ever after. As long as I can pay my bills each month, however, I'll just read about it on the internet.

Sign of the Times

Signs are big business. Almost every business needs a sign, whether it be for advertisement, for directions, to deter loitering, or a simple "Yes, We're Open" sign. And the computer age has brought on an onslaught of graphic sign makers, designers, and artisans making everything from plastic, vinyl, to neon wonders.

But in Fort Payne, there remains throughout the entire town remnants of a legend who defied the odds and advancements of technology and time. His name is Jim Richardson.

If that name sounds familiar, you've no doubt seen the name "Richardson Signs" painted at the bottom of many a plywood signs throughout the area, maybe in the very parking lot where you work, or shop, or tan, or buy flowers, or visit your doctor.

After suffering a mild heart attack, Mr. Richardson retired in 2011 after hand painting signs for over 61 years in the town of Fort Payne. That's not a typo—61 years. That means he started making signs in Fort Payne 14 years before I was born.

If you walk up close to one of his signs, you might notice the faint lines he added to keep the words straight. He still used a brush and paint and did every letter freehand. That's just amazing to me.

I wish I knew more about his background to make this article complete, but perhaps others can write in to the paper or on Facebook and fill in the blanks. The little I know about this incredible guy comes from one visit to his shop about 28 years ago, when I was attending Northeast Community College and stopped by one summer to see if he was hiring.

I didn't get a job, but he was such a nice person, what I got was hours of friendly and interesting conversation. I learned that he wasn't from Alabama at all but met a woman from the area here during World War II and came here to marry her after the war. Falling in love with the place, he stayed.

That's not all I learned about the man on that visit. While I was there, a local politician came in and needed a slew of signs for his campaign. When Mr. Richardson explained that he had many signs to do, but would gladly do the politician's signs in the order it was placed, the politician let him know that he could pay him extra to move him to the front of the line.

Mr. Richardson calmly replied, "I don't need your money. You're not any more important than anyone else. Your signs will be completed in order."

I was in awe. Not only was this man polite, friendly, interesting, and full of great stories; it seems he was made of grit and integrity as well. I hope he's enjoying retirement.

Shade Tree Maniacs

Cars today have complex computer systems that require a lot of training and equipment to adequately repair, but back when I was younger, shade tree mechanics were all over the area. Seeing someone hoisting a motor out of a car using the lowest hanging limb of the tree in their front yard was a common sight.

These men were mechanical wizards who could rebuild a motor or transmission during one weekend and still get in a few hours of fishing. It was nothing for a guy to live in a $20,000 home and have $100,000 worth of tools in his shed.

Bill Dawson, James Dawson's dad (James went to high school with me), could repair any car in the world… well, as long as it was a 1972 Nova. But I think he could build one of those out of three sheets of tin and an old TV antenna. Back in the day, great mechanics on the mountain were a dime a dozen

My dad, however, was not one of them. Dad had his talents, like cooking for one. He learned to cook in the army. His breakfasts were legendary and his chili was second to none. He was also a mathematical genius who, if he'd been given the opportunity, could probably compete with Stephen Hawking.

When it came to cars, however, he was as lost as a blind man in a dark cave on the largest moon of Jupiter. Dad's tools consisted of one set of Vice Grips, one bent Phillips Screwdriver, and a dozen rolls of duct tape. And the tape was the only thing he ever used.

Dad didn't even believe in regular maintenance. I don't know if he ever in his life checked the oil level, transmission fluid, coolant, or even tire pressure for that matter. He would buy a clunker for a few hundred bucks, drive it for a year or two until it conked out, then park it in the front yard and go buy another.

Like most diapers and cigarette lighters, Dad's cars were disposable. When the yard became so crowded that we had nowhere to park the one running vehicle, Dad would sell all of the old cars for scrap and some guy would come and haul them away. Then the process would begin all over again.

You've probably heard the Jeff Foxworthy joke that says, "If you mow your front yard and find a car, you might be a redneck."

That didn't apply to us. With us, it would be more accurate to say, "If you move a car in your front yard and find a patch of grass, you might be a redneck."

A World of Wonder

I was four years old when Neil Armstrong set foot on the moon. It was a fabulous era. On Earth there were all kinds of things happening too. I was mesmerized by toys like the Etch-a-Sketch, Magic 8 Ball, Lite Bright, Spirograph, the Evel Knievel motorcycle, or that game where you tried to take body parts out of the guy without touching the metal sides.

I had a couple of friends who had the coolest thing in their homes. It was a rotary phone, much like ours, but it hung on the wall and had a long curly cord that would allow someone to walk into another room and still converse. I couldn't even imagine having that kind of freedom.

My aunt in Fort Payne, Ester Layfield, had this awesome contraption in the window of her living room. It was basically a big metal box with a fake-wood front, and cold air blew through the vents. I'm not making this up. You could hang meat in there. Every time we visited in the summer, I didn't want to leave.

The summer I turned 13, Junior Winkles gave me my first job outside of a potato shed. He drove a Coca-Cola truck and I worked with him all summer on his route. He would pick me up every day in a brand new, small, black Toyota pickup truck. As he drove, he would push a button on the steering wheel and it would maintain the speed without having to depress the gas pedal.

Right out of high school I was dating this gal from Fort Payne and I loved going to her house because of a gizmo they owned. It was an electronic box that sat on top of their TV. Beside the TV was a box full of flat plastic containers about the size of an album, and inside was a vinyl disc like an album, and you slid one in and it played a movie. Halfway through the movie you had to flip it over to play the rest.

I was a sophomore at Auburn University the first time I witnessed this new-age marvel. I was pulling an all-nighter at Dudley Hall, sitting in the student lounge, when this student took a small bag over to the microwave. Within a minute the entire room smelled like a movie theater lobby. I kid you not; he cooked a bag of popcorn right there. It was more awesome than Jiffy Pop.

Imagine what I thought the first time I saw someone change TV channels with a small box, or saw a calculator on a watch. I have witnessed some amazing stuff, or maybe I'm just easily impressed.

Fearless Findley

It was a fluke, or perhaps irony or fate. I emailed Sylvania Mayor Gerald Craig Monday, September 25th, to ask if he knew who owned the old building where Findley's Groceries used to be, and if it was for sale or lease. I did not know that Pete Findley had passed away that very day.

95

I have such fond memories of that store and the owners. It was our main source of groceries and you were sure to be treated with dignity and respect... and most often a joke. Pete had a great sense of humor.

One memory I have is when my little brother was only about three years old and had picked up a very bad word, a word that means "manure." As Mom was checking out, Pete looked at my brother and said, "What's your name, little man?" My brother blurted out his newfound word and I thought Pete would never stop laughing.

Another memory I have is when Pete caught a young fellow trying to steal a candy bar. Pete just smiled as he spoke kindly to the boy and said, "If you don't have the money for it, go ahead and pay me when you can." The boy took out money, paid for it, and apologized.

Pete had the ability to make people feel appreciated and he treated everyone the same. He will surely be missed. Mayor Craig sent me this tribute below and I wanted to share it in this article because it sums up the man better than I can.

From Sylvania Mayor Gerald Craig: DeKalb County and Sylvania in particular lost a good friend to all who knew him on Monday September 25th, 2017. Moses M. Findley, known of course as "Pete," succumbed to the ravages of Alzheimer's disease after a long struggle.

He and wife, Wanda owned and operated Findley Grocery in Sylvania from the 1970s until the late 1990s when they retired. During those years they were known for their kindness and generosity to all who entered their store. Very few solicitations from school-related activities went unfulfilled and some of those came from schools far removed from where Sylvania buses ran. No one claiming hunger or inability to pay was turned down either.

For several years Pete was a football prognosticator as one of several who picked their slate of winners and losers for a local newspaper. Pete's moniker for that role was "Fearless Findley." He enjoyed that assignment as did the readers. If all his picks had been accurate, the Rams would've had at least ten undefeated seasons.

The Sylvania community mourns with Wanda, David, Angela, and the rest of the family. We will miss him too.

Mr. Niblett Said

No other words made my dad cringe more than when a sentence began with "Mr. Niblett said…" Dad's face would turn red (well, more red than it normally stayed), his jaw muscles would clinch, and his eyes would begin to roll before the sentence was complete.

My two older sisters had Mr. Niblett for science at Sylvania years before I did, so by the time I had him, Dad had already heard all the scientific nonsense he could stand. He just didn't accept that hot water froze faster than cold water, the tongue is the strongest muscle in the human body, or that you can power your home with an electric eel.

But that was the kind of teacher Mr. Niblett was. While other teachers were trying to force you to learn their curriculum by explaining how important it was, or how you will end up on skid row if you didn't learn it, Mr. Niblett's approach was a tad more bizarre. He made it fun

I remember walking into his class one day and there was a ping pong ball levitating in midair. I remember when we boiled water in a paper cup. I remember when we separated the oxygen and hydrogen from water. I remember how he would have everyone get into a circle and hold hands as he was rewinding a film and make static electricity go all the way around and come out the other end.

During my stint in Corporate America, I learned that the best way to instruct an employee was to show them, not to tell them. That's why Mr. Niblett's class was so effective because it was all show and he was the ultimate showman. He didn't simply tell you the properties of centrifugal force; he put you in his desk chair and spun you around until you lost your lunch.

I think most people get into teaching because they love it and want to make a difference. I know it can't be the money. And Terry Niblett sure seemed to enjoy it. He brought a youthful exuberance to the classroom that was contagious. Like that one and only one time he drew a perfect circle on the chalkboard, which I'm guessing he did a hundred times in his tenure.

I think any student who ever had Mr. Niblett was blessed. The experiments, films, and field trips added to the enjoyment. But as society and our youth evolve, I doubt there could be a teacher like him today. I think it took a certain era when kids still respected their teachers and feared their parents.

It's sad that students today will never know the thrill of irking their parents with "Mr. Niblett said…"

Ain't Nuthin' To Do

I used to love going to Desoto Falls on those beautiful spring and summer days. But as I would scan the many cars there, I rarely saw a local license plate. I never could understand how a place so incredible and nearby could be so taken for granted.

I must have heard this phrase a thousand times growing up— "Ain't nuthin' to do around here." But the fact is, nuthin' could be further from the truth. Right there in DeKalb County is the best place in the world to live for something to do.

Okay, granted, there might be more to do in New York City or Los Angeles, but I mean the best place to live for something to do and still live in a normal place with normal people.

Love the beach? Not far to drive to Gulf Shores. Love the mountains? The Great Smoky Mountains are just right up the road. If you like rivers, lakes, fishing, hunting, water skiing, snow skiing, hiking, caverns, boating, swimming, kayaking, camping, river boats, hang gliding, etc., you're absolutely covered.

Or if you're as active as I am, then sightseeing is your thing. I love to just drive around Little River Canyon and have picnics at the overlooks. I might even venture to Sequoia Caverns and see me some buffalo and cruise through the tour.

People think I'm pulling their leg when I tell them about Cloudmont Ski resort in Alabama. I've even hit the slopes there a few times myself. Sure, I was wearing camouflage and had a Remington

30.06 strapped to my back while keeping an eye out for deer, but dogonnit, it's real.

If history is your thing, you can't beat the South with more battlefields than you can shake a dang Yankee at. If you haven't seen a Civil War reenactment, you need to go. And if you haven't been to the Hank Williams museum and gravesite in Montgomery, well, you ain't right. Need something with more bite? Then check out the annual Rattlesnake Rodeo in Opp, Alabama.

If amusement parks are your thing, Lake Winnepesukah in Rossville, Georgia can't be beat. If you fancy a little longer drive, Six Flags and giant water parks are calling your name. Feeling a little spaced-out? Then the Space & Rocket Center in Huntsville might be right up your alley. And if you haven't been to the aquarium and IMax theater in Chattanooga, plan a trip.

When it comes to sports, you have it all. Alabama, Auburn, the Lookouts, Braves, and Falcons all are comfortably nearby. So don't sit back and wish you had something to do, get off your keister and go do it.

Chances are you won't even have to drive farther than Kelly Bunch can throw a football.

www.ingramcontent.com/pod-product-compliance
Lightning Source LLC
Chambersburg PA
CBHW020950030426
42339CB00004B/33